C-143   CAREER EXAMINATION SERIES

This is your
PASSBOOK for...

Clerk-Carrier (USPS)

Test Preparation Study Guide
Questions & Answers

COPYRIGHT NOTICE

This book is SOLELY intended for, is sold ONLY to, and its use is RESTRICTED to individual, bona fide applicants or candidates who qualify by virtue of having seriously filed applications for appropriate license, certificate, professional and/or promotional advancement, higher school matriculation, scholarship, or other legitimate requirements of education and/or governmental authorities.

This book is NOT intended for use, class instruction, tutoring, training, duplication, copying, reprinting, excerption, or adaptation, etc., by:

1) Other publishers
2) Proprietors and/or Instructors of "Coaching" and/or Preparatory Courses
3) Personnel and/or Training Divisions of commercial, industrial, and governmental organizations
4) Schools, colleges, or universities and/or their departments and staffs, including teachers and other personnel
5) Testing Agencies or Bureaus
6) Study groups which seek by the purchase of a single volume to copy and/or duplicate and/or adapt this material for use by the group as a whole without having purchased individual volumes for each of the members of the group
7) Et al.

Such persons would be in violation of appropriate Federal and State statutes.

PROVISION OF LICENSING AGREEMENTS – Recognized educational, commercial, industrial, and governmental institutions and organizations, and others legitimately engaged in educational pursuits, including training, testing, and measurement activities, may address request for a licensing agreement to the copyright owners, who will determine whether, and under what conditions, including fees and charges, the materials in this book may be used them. In other words, a licensing facility exists for the legitimate use of the material in this book on other than an individual basis. However, it is asseverated and affirmed here that the material in this book CANNOT be used without the receipt of the express permission of such a licensing agreement from the Publishers. Inquiries re licensing should be addressed to the company, attention rights and permissions department.

All rights reserved, including the right of reproduction in whole or in part, in any form or by any means, electronic or mechanical, including photocopying, recording, or by any information storage and retrieval system, without permission in writing from the Publisher.

Copyright © 2025 by
National Learning Corporation

212 Michael Drive, Syosset, NY 11791
(516) 921-8888 • www.passbooks.com
E-mail: info@passbooks.com

PASSBOOK® SERIES

THE *PASSBOOK® SERIES* has been created to prepare applicants and candidates for the ultimate academic battlefield – the examination room.

At some time in our lives, each and every one of us may be required to take an examination – for validation, matriculation, admission, qualification, registration, certification, or licensure.

Based on the assumption that every applicant or candidate has met the basic formal educational standards, has taken the required number of courses, and read the necessary texts, the *PASSBOOK® SERIES* furnishes the one special preparation which may assure passing with confidence, instead of failing with insecurity. Examination questions – together with answers – are furnished as the basic vehicle for study so that the mysteries of the examination and its compounding difficulties may be eliminated or diminished by a sure method.

This book is meant to help you pass your examination provided that you qualify and are serious in your objective.

The entire field is reviewed through the huge store of content information which is succinctly presented through a provocative and challenging approach – the question-and-answer method.

A climate of success is established by furnishing the correct answers at the end of each test.

You soon learn to recognize types of questions, forms of questions, and patterns of questioning. You may even begin to anticipate expected outcomes.

You perceive that many questions are repeated or adapted so that you can gain acute insights, which may enable you to score many sure points.

You learn how to confront new questions, or types of questions, and to attack them confidently and work out the correct answers.

You note objectives and emphases, and recognize pitfalls and dangers, so that you may make positive educational adjustments.

Moreover, you are kept fully informed in relation to new concepts, methods, practices, and directions in the field.

You discover that you are actually taking the examination all the time: you are preparing for the examination by "taking" an examination, not by reading extraneous and/or supererogatory textbooks.

In short, this PASSBOOK®, used directedly, should be an important factor in helping you to pass your test.

CLERK CARRIER (U.S.P.S)

DUTIES:

Clerks handle heavy sacks of letter mail, paper mail, and parcel post weighing up to 80 pounds; and sort and distribute mail to post offices and to carrier routes in accordance with established schemes. They may also perform a variety of services at public windows of post offices, post office branches or stations; and perform related duties as assigned. The work involves continuous standing, throwing of mail, stretching, and reaching.

Carriers are responsible for the prompt and efficient delivery and collection of mail on foot or by vehicle under varying conditions in a prescribed area or on various routes. They must serve in all kinds of weather and may be required to drive motor vehicles in all kinds of traffic and road conditions and to deliver parcel post from trucks and make collections of mail from various boxes in the city. They may be required to carry on their shoulders loads weighing as much as 35 pounds and to load and unload full sacks of mail weighing up to 80 pounds from trucks.

The duties of newly appointed Substitute Clerks and Carriers are at times interchangeable. As representatives of the postal service, they must maintain pleasant and effective public relations with patrons and others, requiring a general familiarity with postal laws, regulations, and procedures commonly used, and with the geography of the area.

Male and female employees will be, required to perform the same duties.

EXAMPLES OF TYPICAL TASKS:
- Answer questions about office hours and when items are picked up to be mailed.
- Sell postage and books of stamps.
- Affix stamps to packages.
- Inform customer about postage rates.
- Open post office boxes.
- Retrieve parcels from the back that couldn't be dropped off and give to customer.
- Assist mail carriers by putting mail in bags for transport.
- Sort outgoing mail.
- Check packages for proper postage and addresses.
- Complete forms regarding changes of address, or theft or loss of mail, or for special services such as registered or priority mail.
- Hand-stamp mail.
- Fill out and process money orders.
- Take passport photos and process applications.
- Obtain signatures for priority pick-up.
- Register, certify, and insure letters and parcels.
- Record and balance cash drawer.
- Give change to customers.
- Set postage meters.
- Cash money orders.
- Handle complaints regarding mail theft, delivery problems, and lost or damaged mail.
- Send out notifications for packages that could not be delivered.

WHAT IS THIS BOOK ALL ABOUT?

This book will give you a good idea of what you have to do when you take the Civil Service tests for jobs in the Post Office.

- —It shows how to apply for the test.
- —It explains how to do the different kinds of questions.
- —It describes how to mark your answers on the answer sheet.
- —It gives some of each kind of question to try.
- —Finally, it gives you a chance to test yourself with tests just like those used in the examination—same kinds of questions, same difficulty, same length.

The material is arranged so that you can study by yourself. Read the explanation, try the questions, check your answers. For the questions you get wrong, try to figure out why the correct answer is right and why you made a mistake. If you are working by yourself and you can't figure out why the correct answer is right, try to get some help. Ask a teacher; a librarian; perhaps a brother, a sister, or friend who has gone to high school.

SO YOU WANT TO WORK FOR THE POST OFFICE

THAT'S GREAT!

But... Did You Know

- You have to be 18 or over (16 if you are a high school graduate)
- You have to pass a physical examination
- You have to be a United States citizen
- YOU HAVE TO PASS A CIVIL SERVICE TEST

You will find in this book tests that are very much like the tests you have to take to get a job in the Post Office.

READ AND STUDY THIS BOOK CAREFULLY.

HERE ARE SOME POST OFFICE JOBS

- You could be a MAIL HANDLER.
  You would help move the mail (it's heavy) within the Post Office building.

- You could be a DISTRIBUTION CLERK.
  You would sort the mail (in some places by hand, in some places by machine) and do other things to keep the mail moving

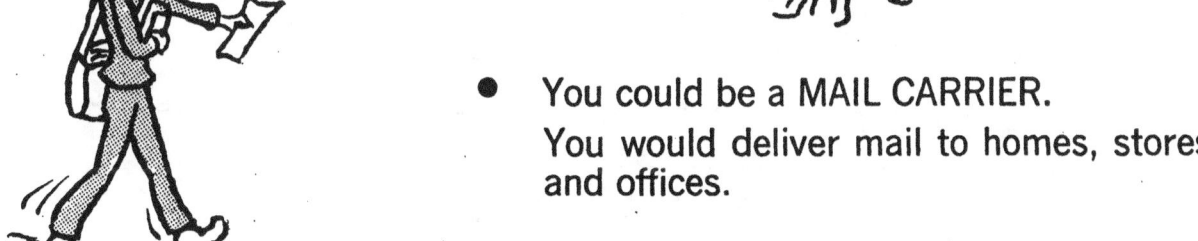

- You could be a MAIL CARRIER.
  You would deliver mail to homes, stores, and offices.

YOU MUST TAKE AND PASS A CIVIL SERVICE TEST IN ORDER TO BE HIRED FOR ANY OF THESE JOBS.

(There are sometimes openings for DRIVERS and GARAGEMEN. There are not many of these jobs, but it's worth checking with your local Post Office or the Federal Job Information Center if you're interested.)

How Do You Apply for a Post Office Job?

FIRST: Go to your nearest Post Office or Federal Job Information Center. Tell them you want to apply for a Post Office job. You will get a form to fill out.

(If they are not accepting applications now, find out when they expect to accept them again. It might be a good idea to start getting ready for the examination anyway.)

You can find the address of your nearest Post Office or Federal Job Information Center in the telephone book.

When you get this form, be sure to find out WHEN you have to send it in, and WHERE you send it.

SECOND: Look over the form. If you don't know how to answer all the questions, ask someone in the office or someone you know for help. If there is no one to help you,

- Answer all the questions the best you can.
- Be sure to print your name and address.

This is what the Application Form looks like

THIRD: Mail the form as soon as you can. (Part of it will be returned to you, telling you when and where to report for the test.)

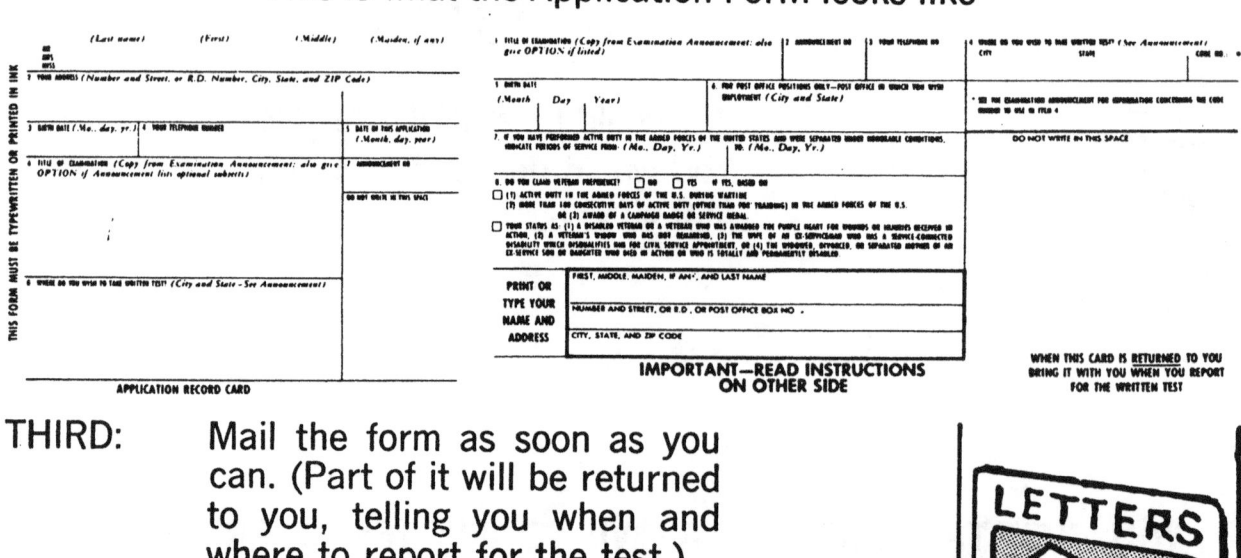

After You Send in Your Application Form

You have mailed in your application form. Soon, you will get back the part that tells you when and where to take the Civil Service test. This is called your admission card. It looks like this:

1. TITLE OF EXAMINATION (Copy from Examination Announcement; also give OPTION if listed)	2. ANNOUNCEMENT NO.	3. YOUR TELEPHONE NO.	4. WHERE DO YOU WISH TO TAKE WRITTEN TEST? (See Announcement) CITY STATE CODE NO.:
5. BIRTH DATE (Month Day Year)	6. FOR POST OFFICE POSITIONS ONLY—POST OFFICE IN WHICH YOU WISH EMPLOYMENT (City and State)		* SEE THE EXAMINATION ANNOUNCEMENT FOR INFORMATION CONCERNING THE CODE NUMBER TO USE IN ITEM 4.
7. IF YOU HAVE PERFORMED ACTIVE DUTY IN THE ARMED FORCES OF THE UNITED STATES AND WERE SEPARATED UNDER HONORABLE CONDITIONS, INDICATE PERIODS OF SERVICE FROM: (Mo., Day, Yr.) TO: (Mo., Day, Yr.)			DO NOT WRITE IN THIS SPACE
8. DO YOU CLAIM VETERAN PREFERENCE? ☐ NO ☐ YES IF YES, BASED ON: ☐ (1) ACTIVE DUTY IN THE ARMED FORCES OF THE U.S. DURING WARTIME (2) MORE THAN 180 CONSECUTIVE DAYS OF ACTIVE DUTY (OTHER THAN FOR TRAINING) IN THE ARMED FORCES OF THE U.S. OR (3) AWARD OF A CAMPAIGN BADGE OR SERVICE MEDAL. ☐ YOUR STATUS AS: (1) A DISABLED VETERAN OR A VETERAN WHO WAS AWARDED THE PURPLE HEART FOR WOUNDS OR INJURIES RECEIVED IN ACTION, (2) A VETERAN'S WIDOW WHO HAS NOT REMARRIED, (3) THE WIFE OF AN EX-SERVICEMAN WHO HAS A SERVICE-CONNECTED DISABILITY WHICH DISQUALIFIES HIM FOR CIVIL SERVICE APPOINTMENT, OR (4) THE WIDOWED, DIVORCED, OR SEPARATED MOTHER OF AN EX-SERVICE SON OR DAUGHTER WHO DIED IN ACTION OR WHO IS TOTALLY AND PERMANENTLY DISABLED.			You will be told here where and when to report for your test.
PRINT OR TYPE YOUR NAME AND ADDRESS	FIRST, MIDDLE, MAIDEN, IF ANY, AND LAST NAME / NUMBER AND STREET, OR R.D., OR POST OFFICE BOX NO. / CITY, STATE, AND ZIP CODE		

IMPORTANT—READ INSTRUCTIONS ON OTHER SIDE

WHEN THIS CARD IS RETURNED TO YOU BRING IT WITH YOU WHEN YOU REPORT FOR THE WRITTEN TEST

Of course, if you did not put down your correct address, or if you forgot to put in your name, you will not hear from anybody.

DO IT RIGHT.

. . . DON'T GET JITTERY JUST BECAUSE
YOU HAVE TO TAKE A TEST.

Go over the tests in this book as carefully as you can. This will help you get ready to take the real test.

AND REMEMBER WHEN YOU SHOW UP

- Be Sure You Have Had A Good Night's Sleep

- Be On Time

- Bring Your Admission Card

IF YOU FORGET TO BRING YOUR ADMISSION CARD, YOU WILL HAVE TO COME BACK ANOTHER TIME, DON'T FORGET

GOOD LUCK...

HOW TO MARK YOUR ANSWER SHEET

The Answer Sheet is where you mark your answers. Your score on the test depends on the marks you make on your Answer Sheet. Therefore, you must mark it exactly the way you are told in the examination room. Some advice on how to use the Answer Sheet is given on this page.

On the next page, you see what a whole Answer Sheet looks like.
Notice how the numbers on the Answer Sheet run across the page—like this:

Your answer mark should look LIKE THIS ⟶ ▮
A neat, heavy line, inside the box.

Do NOT mark your answers like this ⟶ ✗ or ⊘ or ╱ or ▆

Don't take a long time to make your marks. Make a heavy pencil mark and move on to the next question.

For practice, mark the boxes for the following number-letter combinations on the Answer Sheet on the next page. The first four in PART A have been done to show how; you do the rest of PART A—

PART A—1A 2A 3D 4A 5D 6A 7D 8A 9A 10D 11D
12A 13A 14A 15D 16D

Now mark the boxes for the following number-letter combinations in PART B.

PART B—1B 2C 3A 4D 5E 6E 7A 8E 9D 10D 11B
12C 13C 14D 15E

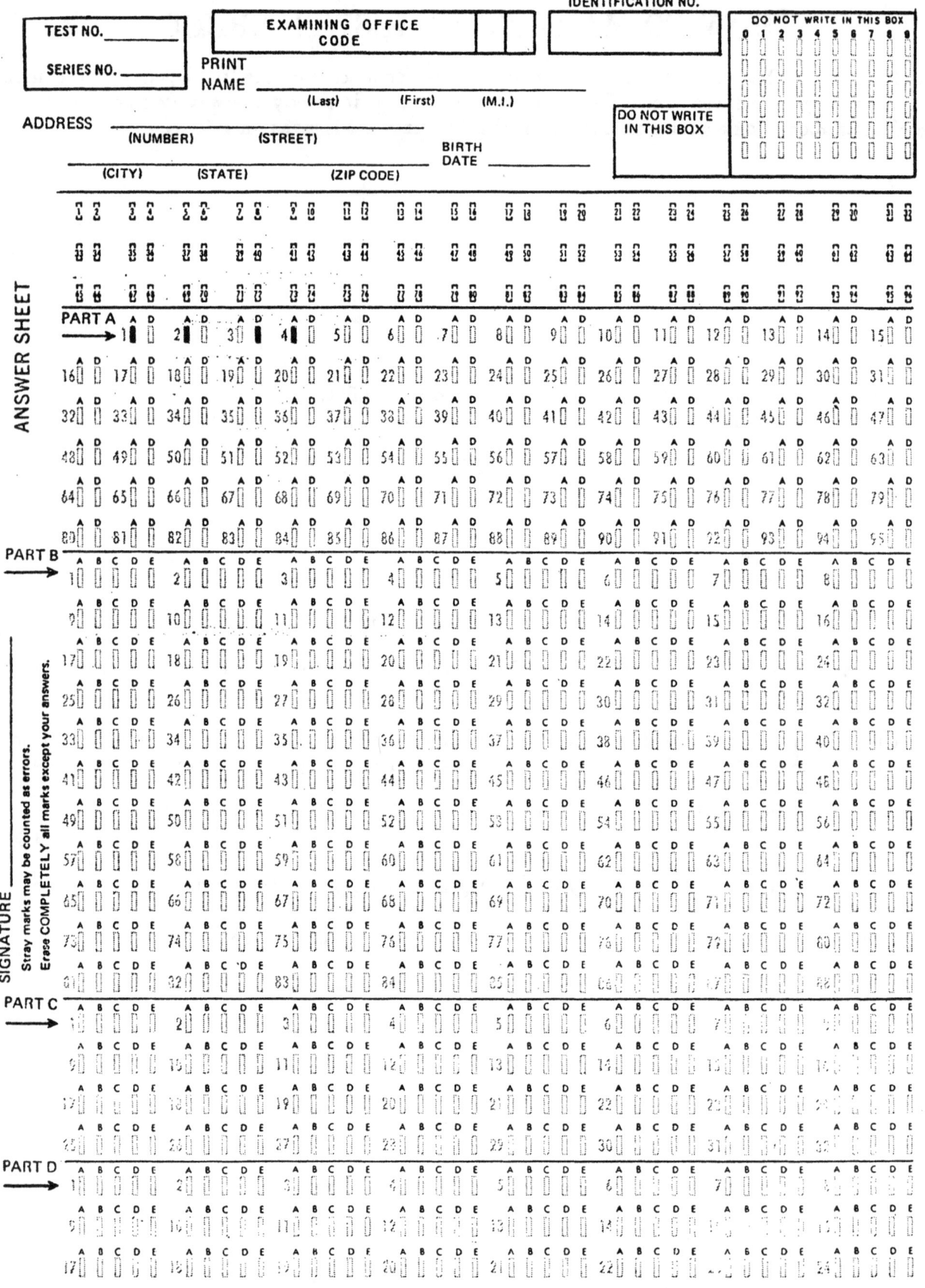

WHAT IS IN THE EXAMINATION

Clerk-Carrier Examination

The test for Clerk-Carrier has four parts. They are:

Part A: Address Checking

> How quickly can you spot whether two addresses are alike or different? This test is harder than the one for the Mail Handler. See practice questions and tests

Part B: Memory for Addresses

> How well can you memorize several groups of names and locations? See practice questions and test

Part C: Word Meaning and Reading

> *Word Meaning*—How well do you understand words you might have to read on the job? See practice questions and test

> *Reading*—How well do you understand the meaning of paragraphs that you are asked to read. See practice questions and tests

Part D: Number Series

> How well can you discover the relationship between numbers in a series? See practice questions and tests

After you have passed this test, you will be placed on a list of eligibles on the basis of your score. If you are entitled to veterans' preference, you will be given the extra credit. (The higher your score the nearer the top of the list you will be.)

NOTE:

The *full* written test for the Clerk-Carrier examination consists of the four (4) parts listed above. However, in recent years, the United States Postal Service, in accordance with staffing needs and conditions, has been offering only three of these parts on the Clerk-Carrier written examination. Therefore, be sure to check the Official Announcement before *you* take *your* test.

Study only the sections in this book on which you will be tested. If all four, study the entire book. If three, study only those three sections.

PRACTICE TESTS

How To Use These Practice Tests

On the following pages, you will find questions just like the ones used in the Civil Service examinations for these jobs in the post office. Each type of question is explained separately. Study the sample and then do the practice tests.

Each practice test is timed. Have a friend watch the time for you.

When you have finished each practice test, go back and check your answers to find out what your score is. Then compare your score with the scale that goes with the test to determine how well you did. This will help you to find out where you need more practice.

Be sure to do the Practice Tests before you attempt the Sample Test at the back. These tests are exactly like the ones you will have to take in the examinations. The time limit for each part and the type of questions in each part are exactly like they are in the Civil Service examinations.

HOW TO TAKE A TEST

I. YOU MUST PASS AN EXAMINATION

A. WHAT EVERY CANDIDATE SHOULD KNOW

Examination applicants often ask us for help in preparing for the written test. What can I study in advance? What kinds of questions will be asked? How will the test be given? How will the papers be graded?

As an applicant for a civil service examination, you may be wondering about some of these things. Our purpose here is to suggest effective methods of advance study and to describe civil service examinations.

Your chances for success on this examination can be increased if you know how to prepare. Those "pre-examination jitters" can be reduced if you know what to expect. You can even experience an adventure in good citizenship if you know why civil service exams are given.

B. WHY ARE CIVIL SERVICE EXAMINATIONS GIVEN?

Civil service examinations are important to you in two ways. As a citizen, you want public jobs filled by employees who know how to do their work. As a job seeker, you want a fair chance to compete for that job on an equal footing with other candidates. The best-known means of accomplishing this two-fold goal is the competitive examination.

Exams are widely publicized throughout the nation. They may be administered for jobs in federal, state, city, municipal, town or village governments or agencies.

Any citizen may apply, with some limitations, such as the age or residence of applicants. Your experience and education may be reviewed to see whether you meet the requirements for the particular examination. When these requirements exist, they are reasonable and applied consistently to all applicants. Thus, a competitive examination may cause you some uneasiness now, but it is your privilege and safeguard.

C. HOW ARE CIVIL SERVICE EXAMS DEVELOPED?

Examinations are carefully written by trained technicians who are specialists in the field known as "psychological measurement," in consultation with recognized authorities in the field of work that the test will cover. These experts recommend the subject matter areas or skills to be tested; only those knowledges or skills important to your success on the job are included. The most reliable books and source materials available are used as references. Together, the experts and technicians judge the difficulty level of the questions.

Test technicians know how to phrase questions so that the problem is clearly stated. Their ethics do not permit "trick" or "catch" questions. Questions may have been tried out on sample groups, or subjected to statistical analysis, to determine their usefulness.

Written tests are often used in combination with performance tests, ratings of training and experience, and oral interviews. All of these measures combine to form the best-known means of finding the right person for the right job.

II. HOW TO PASS THE WRITTEN TEST

A. NATURE OF THE EXAMINATION

To prepare intelligently for civil service examinations, you should know how they differ from school examinations you have taken. In school you were assigned certain definite pages to read or subjects to cover. The examination questions were quite detailed and usually emphasized memory. Civil service exams, on the other hand, try to discover your present ability to perform the duties of a position, plus your potentiality to learn these duties. In other words, a civil service exam attempts to predict how successful you will be. Questions cover such a broad area that they cannot be as minute and detailed as school exam questions.

In the public service similar kinds of work, or positions, are grouped together in one "class." This process is known as *position-classification*. All the positions in a class are paid according to the salary range for that class. One class title covers all of these positions, and they are all tested by the same examination.

B. FOUR BASIC STEPS

1) Study the announcement

How, then, can you know what subjects to study? Our best answer is: "Learn as much as possible about the class of positions for which you've applied." The exam will test the knowledge, skills and abilities needed to do the work.

Your most valuable source of information about the position you want is the official exam announcement. This announcement lists the training and experience qualifications. Check these standards and apply only if you come reasonably close to meeting them.

The brief description of the position in the examination announcement offers some clues to the subjects which will be tested. Think about the job itself. Review the duties in your mind. Can you perform them, or are there some in which you are rusty? Fill in the blank spots in your preparation.

Many jurisdictions preview the written test in the exam announcement by including a section called "Knowledge and Abilities Required," "Scope of the Examination," or some similar heading. Here you will find out specifically what fields will be tested.

2) Review your own background

Once you learn in general what the position is all about, and what you need to know to do the work, ask yourself which subjects you already know fairly well and which need improvement. You may wonder whether to concentrate on improving your strong areas or on building some background in your fields of weakness. When the announcement has specified "some knowledge" or "considerable knowledge," or has used adjectives like "beginning principles of..." or "advanced ... methods," you can get a clue as to the number and difficulty of questions to be asked in any given field. More questions, and hence broader coverage, would be included for those subjects which are more important in the work. Now weigh your strengths and weaknesses against the job requirements and prepare accordingly.

3) Determine the level of the position

Another way to tell how intensively you should prepare is to understand the level of the job for which you are applying. Is it the entering level? In other words, is this the position in which beginners in a field of work are hired? Or is it an intermediate or advanced level? Sometimes this is indicated by such words as "Junior" or "Senior" in the class title. Other jurisdictions use Roman numerals to designate the level – Clerk I, Clerk II, for example. The word "Supervisor" sometimes appears in the title. If the level is not indicated by the title, check the description of duties. Will you be working under very close supervision, or will you have responsibility for independent decisions in this work?

4) Choose appropriate study materials

Now that you know the subjects to be examined and the relative amount of each subject to be covered, you can choose suitable study materials. For beginning level jobs, or even advanced ones, if you have a pronounced weakness in some aspect of your training, read a modern, standard textbook in that field. Be sure it is up to date and has general coverage. Such books are normally available at your library, and the librarian will be glad to help you locate one. For entry-level positions, questions of appropriate difficulty are chosen – neither highly advanced questions, nor those too simple. Such questions require careful thought but not advanced training.

If the position for which you are applying is technical or advanced, you will read more advanced, specialized material. If you are already familiar with the basic principles of your field, elementary textbooks would waste your time. Concentrate on advanced textbooks and technical periodicals. Think through the concepts and review difficult problems in your field.

These are all general sources. You can get more ideas on your own initiative, following these leads. For example, training manuals and publications of the government agency which employs workers in your field can be useful, particularly for technical and professional positions. A letter or visit to the government department involved may result in more specific study suggestions, and certainly will provide you with a more definite idea of the exact nature of the position you are seeking.

III. KINDS OF TESTS

Tests are used for purposes other than measuring knowledge and ability to perform specified duties. For some positions, it is equally important to test ability to make adjustments to new situations or to profit from training. In others, basic mental abilities not dependent on information are essential. Questions which test these things may not appear as pertinent to the duties of the position as those which test for knowledge and information. Yet they are often highly important parts of a fair examination. For very general questions, it is almost impossible to help you direct your study efforts. What we can do is to point out some of the more common of these general abilities needed in public service positions and describe some typical questions.

1) General information

Broad, general information has been found useful for predicting job success in some kinds of work. This is tested in a variety of ways, from vocabulary lists to questions about current events. Basic background in some field of work, such as sociology or economics, may be sampled in a group of questions. Often these are principles which have become familiar to most persons through exposure rather than through formal training. It is difficult to advise you how to study for these questions; being alert to the world around you is our best suggestion.

2) Verbal ability

An example of an ability needed in many positions is verbal or language ability. Verbal ability is, in brief, the ability to use and understand words. Vocabulary and grammar tests are typical measures of this ability. Reading comprehension or paragraph interpretation questions are common in many kinds of civil service tests. You are given a paragraph of written material and asked to find its central meaning.

3) Numerical ability

Number skills can be tested by the familiar arithmetic problem, by checking paired lists of numbers to see which are alike and which are different, or by interpreting charts and graphs. In the latter test, a graph may be printed in the test booklet which you are asked to use as the basis for answering questions.

4) Observation

A popular test for law-enforcement positions is the observation test. A picture is shown to you for several minutes, then taken away. Questions about the picture test your ability to observe both details and larger elements.

5) Following directions

In many positions in the public service, the employee must be able to carry out written instructions dependably and accurately. You may be given a chart with several columns, each column listing a variety of information. The questions require you to carry out directions involving the information given in the chart.

6) Skills and aptitudes

Performance tests effectively measure some manual skills and aptitudes. When the skill is one in which you are trained, such as typing or shorthand, you can practice. These tests are often very much like those given in business school or high school courses. For many of the other skills and aptitudes, however, no short-time preparation can be made. Skills and abilities natural to you or that you have developed throughout your lifetime are being tested.

Many of the general questions just described provide all the data needed to answer the questions and ask you to use your reasoning ability to find the answers. Your best preparation for these tests, as well as for tests of facts and ideas, is to be at your physical and mental best. You, no doubt, have your own methods of getting into an exam-taking mood and keeping "in shape." The next section lists some ideas on this subject.

IV. KINDS OF QUESTIONS

Only rarely is the "essay" question, which you answer in narrative form, used in civil service tests. Civil service tests are usually of the short-answer type. Full instructions for answering these questions will be given to you at the examination. But in case this is your first experience with short-answer questions and separate answer sheets, here is what you need to know:

1) Multiple-choice Questions

Most popular of the short-answer questions is the "multiple choice" or "best answer" question. It can be used, for example, to test for factual knowledge, ability to solve problems or judgment in meeting situations found at work.

A multiple-choice question is normally one of three types—
- It can begin with an incomplete statement followed by several possible endings. You are to find the one ending which *best* completes the statement, although some of the others may not be entirely wrong.
- It can also be a complete statement in the form of a question which is answered by choosing one of the statements listed.

- It can be in the form of a problem – again you select the best answer.

Here is an example of a multiple-choice question with a discussion which should give you some clues as to the method for choosing the right answer:

When an employee has a complaint about his assignment, the action which will *best* help him overcome his difficulty is to
   A. discuss his difficulty with his coworkers
   B. take the problem to the head of the organization
   C. take the problem to the person who gave him the assignment
   D. say nothing to anyone about his complaint

In answering this question, you should study each of the choices to find which is best. Consider choice "A" – Certainly an employee may discuss his complaint with fellow employees, but no change or improvement can result, and the complaint remains unresolved. Choice "B" is a poor choice since the head of the organization probably does not know what assignment you have been given, and taking your problem to him is known as "going over the head" of the supervisor. The supervisor, or person who made the assignment, is the person who can clarify it or correct any injustice. Choice "C" is, therefore, correct. To say nothing, as in choice "D," is unwise. Supervisors have and interest in knowing the problems employees are facing, and the employee is seeking a solution to his problem.

2) True/False Questions

The "true/false" or "right/wrong" form of question is sometimes used. Here a complete statement is given. Your job is to decide whether the statement is right or wrong.

SAMPLE: A roaming cell-phone call to a nearby city costs less than a non-roaming call to a distant city.

This statement is wrong, or false, since roaming calls are more expensive.

This is not a complete list of all possible question forms, although most of the others are variations of these common types. You will always get complete directions for answering questions. Be sure you understand *how* to mark your answers – ask questions until you do.

V. RECORDING YOUR ANSWERS

Computer terminals are used more and more today for many different kinds of exams.

For an examination with very few applicants, you may be told to record your answers in the test booklet itself. Separate answer sheets are much more common. If this separate answer sheet is to be scored by machine – and this is often the case – it is highly important that you mark your answers correctly in order to get credit.

An electronic scoring machine is often used in civil service offices because of the speed with which papers can be scored. Machine-scored answer sheets must be marked with a pencil, which will be given to you. This pencil has a high graphite content which responds to the electronic scoring machine. As a matter of fact, stray dots may register as answers, so do not let your pencil rest on the answer sheet while you are pondering the correct answer. Also, if your pencil lead breaks or is otherwise defective, ask for another.

Since the answer sheet will be dropped in a slot in the scoring machine, be careful not to bend the corners or get the paper crumpled.

The answer sheet normally has five vertical columns of numbers, with 30 numbers to a column. These numbers correspond to the question numbers in your test booklet. After each number, going across the page are four or five pairs of dotted lines. These short dotted lines have small letters or numbers above them. The first two pairs may also have a "T" or "F" above the letters. This indicates that the first two pairs only are to be used if the questions are of the true-false type. If the questions are multiple choice, disregard the "T" and "F" and pay attention only to the small letters or numbers.

Answer your questions in the manner of the sample that follows:

32. The largest city in the United States is
    A. Washington, D.C.
    B. New York City
    C. Chicago
    D. Detroit
    E. San Francisco

1) Choose the answer you think is best. (New York City is the largest, so "B" is correct.)
2) Find the row of dotted lines numbered the same as the question you are answering. (Find row number 32)
3) Find the pair of dotted lines corresponding to the answer. (Find the pair of lines under the mark "B.")
4) Make a solid black mark between the dotted lines.

VI. BEFORE THE TEST

Common sense will help you find procedures to follow to get ready for an examination. Too many of us, however, overlook these sensible measures. Indeed, nervousness and fatigue have been found to be the most serious reasons why applicants fail to do their best on civil service tests. Here is a list of reminders:

- Begin your preparation early – Don't wait until the last minute to go scurrying around for books and materials or to find out what the position is all about.
- Prepare continuously – An hour a night for a week is better than an all-night cram session. This has been definitely established. What is more, a night a week for a month will return better dividends than crowding your study into a shorter period of time.
- Locate the place of the exam – You have been sent a notice telling you when and where to report for the examination. If the location is in a different town or otherwise unfamiliar to you, it would be well to inquire the best route and learn something about the building.
- Relax the night before the test – Allow your mind to rest. Do not study at all that night. Plan some mild recreation or diversion; then go to bed early and get a good night's sleep.
- Get up early enough to make a leisurely trip to the place for the test – This way unforeseen events, traffic snarls, unfamiliar buildings, etc. will not upset you.
- Dress comfortably – A written test is not a fashion show. You will be known by number and not by name, so wear something comfortable.

- Leave excess paraphernalia at home – Shopping bags and odd bundles will get in your way. You need bring only the items mentioned in the official notice you received; usually everything you need is provided. Do not bring reference books to the exam. They will only confuse those last minutes and be taken away from you when in the test room.
- Arrive somewhat ahead of time – If because of transportation schedules you must get there very early, bring a newspaper or magazine to take your mind off yourself while waiting.
- Locate the examination room – When you have found the proper room, you will be directed to the seat or part of the room where you will sit. Sometimes you are given a sheet of instructions to read while you are waiting. Do not fill out any forms until you are told to do so; just read them and be prepared.
- Relax and prepare to listen to the instructions
- If you have any physical problem that may keep you from doing your best, be sure to tell the test administrator. If you are sick or in poor health, you really cannot do your best on the exam. You can come back and take the test some other time.

VII. AT THE TEST

The day of the test is here and you have the test booklet in your hand. The temptation to get going is very strong. Caution! There is more to success than knowing the right answers. You must know how to identify your papers and understand variations in the type of short-answer question used in this particular examination. Follow these suggestions for maximum results from your efforts:

1) Cooperate with the monitor

The test administrator has a duty to create a situation in which you can be as much at ease as possible. He will give instructions, tell you when to begin, check to see that you are marking your answer sheet correctly, and so on. He is not there to guard you, although he will see that your competitors do not take unfair advantage. He wants to help you do your best.

2) Listen to all instructions

Don't jump the gun! Wait until you understand all directions. In most civil service tests you get more time than you need to answer the questions. So don't be in a hurry. Read each word of instructions until you clearly understand the meaning. Study the examples, listen to all announcements and follow directions. Ask questions if you do not understand what to do.

3) Identify your papers

Civil service exams are usually identified by number only. You will be assigned a number; you must not put your name on your test papers. Be sure to copy your number correctly. Since more than one exam may be given, copy your exact examination title.

4) Plan your time

Unless you are told that a test is a "speed" or "rate of work" test, speed itself is usually not important. Time enough to answer all the questions will be provided, but this does not mean that you have all day. An overall time limit has been set. Divide the total time (in minutes) by the number of questions to determine the approximate time you have for each question.

5) Do not linger over difficult questions

If you come across a difficult question, mark it with a paper clip (useful to have along) and come back to it when you have been through the booklet. One caution if you do this – be sure to skip a number on your answer sheet as well. Check often to be sure that you have not lost your place and that you are marking in the row numbered the same as the question you are answering.

6) Read the questions

Be sure you know what the question asks! Many capable people are unsuccessful because they failed to *read* the questions correctly.

7) Answer all questions

Unless you have been instructed that a penalty will be deducted for incorrect answers, it is better to guess than to omit a question.

8) Speed tests

It is often better NOT to guess on speed tests. It has been found that on timed tests people are tempted to spend the last few seconds before time is called in marking answers at random – without even reading them – in the hope of picking up a few extra points. To discourage this practice, the instructions may warn you that your score will be "corrected" for guessing. That is, a penalty will be applied. The incorrect answers will be deducted from the correct ones, or some other penalty formula will be used.

9) Review your answers

If you finish before time is called, go back to the questions you guessed or omitted to give them further thought. Review other answers if you have time.

10) Return your test materials

If you are ready to leave before others have finished or time is called, take ALL your materials to the monitor and leave quietly. Never take any test material with you. The monitor can discover whose papers are not complete, and taking a test booklet may be grounds for disqualification.

VIII. EXAMINATION TECHNIQUES

1) Read the general instructions carefully. These are usually printed on the first page of the exam booklet. As a rule, these instructions refer to the timing of the examination; the fact that you should not start work until the signal and must stop work at a signal, etc. If there are any *special* instructions, such as a choice of questions to be answered, make sure that you note this instruction carefully.

2) When you are ready to start work on the examination, that is as soon as the signal has been given, read the instructions to each question booklet, underline any key words or phrases, such as *least, best, outline, describe* and the like. In this way you will tend to answer as requested rather than discover on reviewing your paper that you *listed without describing*, that you selected the *worst* choice rather than the *best* choice, etc.

3) If the examination is of the objective or multiple-choice type – that is, each question will also give a series of possible answers: A, B, C or D, and you are called upon to select the best answer and write the letter next to that answer on your answer paper – it is advisable to start answering each question in turn. There may be anywhere from 50 to 100 such questions in the three or four hours allotted and you can see how much time would be taken if you read through all the questions before beginning to answer any. Furthermore, if you come across a question or group of questions which you know would be difficult to answer, it would undoubtedly affect your handling of all the other questions.

4) If the examination is of the essay type and contains but a few questions, it is a moot point as to whether you should read all the questions before starting to answer any one. Of course, if you are given a choice – say five out of seven and the like – then it is essential to read all the questions so you can eliminate the two that are most difficult. If, however, you are asked to answer all the questions, there may be danger in trying to answer the easiest one first because you may find that you will spend too much time on it. The best technique is to answer the first question, then proceed to the second, etc.

5) Time your answers. Before the exam begins, write down the time it started, then add the time allowed for the examination and write down the time it must be completed, then divide the time available somewhat as follows:
    - If 3-1/2 hours are allowed, that would be 210 minutes. If you have 80 objective-type questions, that would be an average of 2-1/2 minutes per question. Allow yourself no more than 2 minutes per question, or a total of 160 minutes, which will permit about 50 minutes to review.
    - If for the time allotment of 210 minutes there are 7 essay questions to answer, that would average about 30 minutes a question. Give yourself only 25 minutes per question so that you have about 35 minutes to review.

6) The most important instruction is to *read each question* and make sure you know what is wanted. The second most important instruction is to *time yourself properly* so that you answer every question. The third most important instruction is to *answer every question*. Guess if you have to but include something for each question. Remember that you will receive no credit for a blank and will probably receive some credit if you write something in answer to an essay question. If you guess a letter – say "B" for a multiple-choice question – you may have guessed right. If you leave a blank as an answer to a multiple-choice question, the examiners may respect your feelings but it will not add a point to your score. Some exams may penalize you for wrong answers, so in such cases *only*, you may not want to guess unless you have some basis for your answer.

7) Suggestions
    a. Objective-type questions
        1. Examine the question booklet for proper sequence of pages and questions
        2. Read all instructions carefully
        3. Skip any question which seems too difficult; return to it after all other questions have been answered
        4. Apportion your time properly; do not spend too much time on any single question or group of questions

5. Note and underline key words – *all, most, fewest, least, best, worst, same, opposite,* etc.
6. Pay particular attention to negatives
7. Note unusual option, e.g., unduly long, short, complex, different or similar in content to the body of the question
8. Observe the use of "hedging" words – *probably, may, most likely,* etc.
9. Make sure that your answer is put next to the same number as the question
10. Do not second-guess unless you have good reason to believe the second answer is definitely more correct
11. Cross out original answer if you decide another answer is more accurate; do not erase until you are ready to hand your paper in
12. Answer all questions; guess unless instructed otherwise
13. Leave time for review

b. Essay questions
   1. Read each question carefully
   2. Determine exactly what is wanted. Underline key words or phrases.
   3. Decide on outline or paragraph answer
   4. Include many different points and elements unless asked to develop any one or two points or elements
   5. Show impartiality by giving pros and cons unless directed to select one side only
   6. Make and write down any assumptions you find necessary to answer the questions
   7. Watch your English, grammar, punctuation and choice of words
   8. Time your answers; don't crowd material

8) Answering the essay question

Most essay questions can be answered by framing the specific response around several key words or ideas. Here are a few such key words or ideas:

M's: manpower, materials, methods, money, management
P's: purpose, program, policy, plan, procedure, practice, problems, pitfalls, personnel, public relations

   a. Six basic steps in handling problems:
      1. Preliminary plan and background development
      2. Collect information, data and facts
      3. Analyze and interpret information, data and facts
      4. Analyze and develop solutions as well as make recommendations
      5. Prepare report and sell recommendations
      6. Install recommendations and follow up effectiveness

   b. Pitfalls to avoid
      1. *Taking things for granted* – A statement of the situation does not necessarily imply that each of the elements is necessarily true; for example, a complaint may be invalid and biased so that all that can be taken for granted is that a complaint has been registered

2. *Considering only one side of a situation* – Wherever possible, indicate several alternatives and then point out the reasons you selected the best one
3. *Failing to indicate follow up* – Whenever your answer indicates action on your part, make certain that you will take proper follow-up action to see how successful your recommendations, procedures or actions turn out to be
4. *Taking too long in answering any single question* – Remember to time your answers properly

IX. AFTER THE TEST

Scoring procedures differ in detail among civil service jurisdictions although the general principles are the same. Whether the papers are hand-scored or graded by machine we have described, they are nearly always graded by number. That is, the person who marks the paper knows only the number – never the name – of the applicant. Not until all the papers have been graded will they be matched with names. If other tests, such as training and experience or oral interview ratings have been given, scores will be combined. Different parts of the examination usually have different weights. For example, the written test might count 60 percent of the final grade, and a rating of training and experience 40 percent. In many jurisdictions, veterans will have a certain number of points added to their grades.

After the final grade has been determined, the names are placed in grade order and an eligible list is established. There are various methods for resolving ties between those who get the same final grade – probably the most common is to place first the name of the person whose application was received first. Job offers are made from the eligible list in the order the names appear on it. You will be notified of your grade and your rank as soon as all these computations have been made. This will be done as rapidly as possible.

People who are found to meet the requirements in the announcement are called "eligibles." Their names are put on a list of eligible candidates. An eligible's chances of getting a job depend on how high he stands on this list and how fast agencies are filling jobs from the list.

When a job is to be filled from a list of eligibles, the agency asks for the names of people on the list of eligibles for that job. When the civil service commission receives this request, it sends to the agency the names of the three people highest on this list. Or, if the job to be filled has specialized requirements, the office sends the agency the names of the top three persons who meet these requirements from the general list.

The appointing officer makes a choice from among the three people whose names were sent to him. If the selected person accepts the appointment, the names of the others are put back on the list to be considered for future openings.

That is the rule in hiring from all kinds of eligible lists, whether they are for typist, carpenter, chemist, or something else. For every vacancy, the appointing officer has his choice of any one of the top three eligibles on the list. This explains why the person whose name is on top of the list sometimes does not get an appointment when some of the persons lower on the list do. If the appointing officer chooses the second or third eligible, the No. 1 eligible does not get a job at once, but stays on the list until he is appointed or the list is terminated.

X. HOW TO PASS THE INTERVIEW TEST

The examination for which you applied requires an oral interview test. You have already taken the written test and you are now being called for the interview test – the final part of the formal examination.

You may think that it is not possible to prepare for an interview test and that there are no procedures to follow during an interview. Our purpose is to point out some things you can do in advance that will help you and some good rules to follow and pitfalls to avoid while you are being interviewed.

What is an interview supposed to test?

The written examination is designed to test the technical knowledge and competence of the candidate; the oral is designed to evaluate intangible qualities, not readily measured otherwise, and to establish a list showing the relative fitness of each candidate – as measured against his competitors – for the position sought. Scoring is not on the basis of "right" and "wrong," but on a sliding scale of values ranging from "not passable" to "outstanding." As a matter of fact, it is possible to achieve a relatively low score without a single "incorrect" answer because of evident weakness in the qualities being measured.

Occasionally, an examination may consist entirely of an oral test – either an individual or a group oral. In such cases, information is sought concerning the technical knowledges and abilities of the candidate, since there has been no written examination for this purpose. More commonly, however, an oral test is used to supplement a written examination.

Who conducts interviews?

The composition of oral boards varies among different jurisdictions. In nearly all, a representative of the personnel department serves as chairman. One of the members of the board may be a representative of the department in which the candidate would work. In some cases, "outside experts" are used, and, frequently, a businessman or some other representative of the general public is asked to serve. Labor and management or other special groups may be represented. The aim is to secure the services of experts in the appropriate field.

However the board is composed, it is a good idea (and not at all improper or unethical) to ascertain in advance of the interview who the members are and what groups they represent. When you are introduced to them, you will have some idea of their backgrounds and interests, and at least you will not stutter and stammer over their names.

What should be done before the interview?

While knowledge about the board members is useful and takes some of the surprise element out of the interview, there is other preparation which is more substantive. It *is* possible to prepare for an oral interview – in several ways:

1) Keep a copy of your application and review it carefully before the interview

This may be the only document before the oral board, and the starting point of the interview. Know what education and experience you have listed there, and the sequence and dates of all of it. Sometimes the board will ask you to review the highlights of your experience for them; you should not have to hem and haw doing it.

2) Study the class specification and the examination announcement

Usually, the oral board has one or both of these to guide them. The qualities, characteristics or knowledges required by the position sought are stated in these documents. They offer valuable clues as to the nature of the oral interview. For example, if the job involves supervisory responsibilities, the announcement will usually indicate that knowledge of modern supervisory methods and the qualifications of the candidate as a supervisor will be tested. If so, you can expect such questions, frequently in the form of a hypothetical situation which you are expected to solve. NEVER go into an oral without knowledge of the duties and responsibilities of the job you seek.

3) Think through each qualification required

Try to visualize the kind of questions you would ask if you were a board member. How well could you answer them? Try especially to appraise your own knowledge and background in each area, *measured against the job sought*, and identify any areas in which you are weak. Be critical and realistic – do not flatter yourself.

4) Do some general reading in areas in which you feel you may be weak

For example, if the job involves supervision and your past experience has NOT, some general reading in supervisory methods and practices, particularly in the field of human relations, might be useful. Do NOT study agency procedures or detailed manuals. The oral board will be testing your understanding and capacity, not your memory.

5) Get a good night's sleep and watch your general health and mental attitude

You will want a clear head at the interview. Take care of a cold or any other minor ailment, and of course, no hangovers.

What should be done on the day of the interview?

Now comes the day of the interview itself. Give yourself plenty of time to get there. Plan to arrive somewhat ahead of the scheduled time, particularly if your appointment is in the fore part of the day. If a previous candidate fails to appear, the board might be ready for you a bit early. By early afternoon an oral board is almost invariably behind schedule if there are many candidates, and you may have to wait. Take along a book or magazine to read, or your application to review, but leave any extraneous material in the waiting room when you go in for your interview. In any event, relax and compose yourself.

The matter of dress is important. The board is forming impressions about you – from your experience, your manners, your attitude, and your appearance. Give your personal appearance careful attention. Dress your best, but not your flashiest. Choose conservative, appropriate clothing, and be sure it is immaculate. This is a business interview, and your appearance should indicate that you regard it as such. Besides, being well groomed and properly dressed will help boost your confidence.

Sooner or later, someone will call your name and escort you into the interview room. *This is it.* From here on you are on your own. It is too late for any more preparation. But remember, you asked for this opportunity to prove your fitness, and you are here because your request was granted.

What happens when you go in?

The usual sequence of events will be as follows: The clerk (who is often the board stenographer) will introduce you to the chairman of the oral board, who will introduce you to the other members of the board. Acknowledge the introductions before you sit down. Do not be surprised if you find a microphone facing you or a stenotypist sitting by. Oral interviews are usually recorded in the event of an appeal or other review.

Usually the chairman of the board will open the interview by reviewing the highlights of your education and work experience from your application – primarily for the benefit of the other members of the board, as well as to get the material into the record. Do not interrupt or comment unless there is an error or significant misinterpretation; if that is the case, do not hesitate. But do not quibble about insignificant matters. Also, he will usually ask you some question about your education, experience or your present job – partly to get you to start talking and to establish the interviewing "rapport." He may start the actual questioning, or turn it over to one of the other members. Frequently, each member undertakes the questioning on a particular area, one in which he is perhaps most competent, so you can expect each member to participate in the examination. Because time is limited, you may also expect some rather abrupt switches in the direction the questioning takes, so do not be upset by it. Normally, a board member will not pursue a single line of questioning unless he discovers a particular strength or weakness.

After each member has participated, the chairman will usually ask whether any member has any further questions, then will ask you if you have anything you wish to add. Unless you are expecting this question, it may floor you. Worse, it may start you off on an extended, extemporaneous speech. The board is not usually seeking more information. The question is principally to offer you a last opportunity to present further qualifications or to indicate that you have nothing to add. So, if you feel that a significant qualification or characteristic has been overlooked, it is proper to point it out in a sentence or so. Do not compliment the board on the thoroughness of their examination – they have been sketchy, and you know it. If you wish, merely say, "No thank you, I have nothing further to add." This is a point where you can "talk yourself out" of a good impression or fail to present an important bit of information. Remember, *you close the interview yourself.*

The chairman will then say, "That is all, Mr. _____, thank you." Do not be startled; the interview is over, and quicker than you think. Thank him, gather your belongings and take your leave. Save your sigh of relief for the other side of the door.

How to put your best foot forward
Throughout this entire process, you may feel that the board individually and collectively is trying to pierce your defenses, seek out your hidden weaknesses and embarrass and confuse you. Actually, this is not true. They are obliged to make an appraisal of your qualifications for the job you are seeking, and they want to see you in your best light. Remember, they must interview all candidates and a non-cooperative candidate may become a failure in spite of their best efforts to bring out his qualifications. Here are 15 suggestions that will help you:

1) Be natural – Keep your attitude confident, not cocky
If you are not confident that you can do the job, do not expect the board to be. Do not apologize for your weaknesses, try to bring out your strong points. The board is interested in a positive, not negative, presentation. Cockiness will antagonize any board member and make him wonder if you are covering up a weakness by a false show of strength.

2) Get comfortable, but don't lounge or sprawl
Sit erectly but not stiffly. A careless posture may lead the board to conclude that you are careless in other things, or at least that you are not impressed by the importance of the occasion. Either conclusion is natural, even if incorrect. Do not fuss with your clothing, a pencil or an ashtray. Your hands may occasionally be useful to emphasize a point; do not let them become a point of distraction.

3) Do not wisecrack or make small talk
This is a serious situation, and your attitude should show that you consider it as such. Further, the time of the board is limited – they do not want to waste it, and neither should you.

4) Do not exaggerate your experience or abilities

In the first place, from information in the application or other interviews and sources, the board may know more about you than you think. Secondly, you probably will not get away with it. An experienced board is rather adept at spotting such a situation, so do not take the chance.

5) If you know a board member, do not make a point of it, yet do not hide it

Certainly you are not fooling him, and probably not the other members of the board. Do not try to take advantage of your acquaintanceship – it will probably do you little good.

6) Do not dominate the interview

Let the board do that. They will give you the clues – do not assume that you have to do all the talking. Realize that the board has a number of questions to ask you, and do not try to take up all the interview time by showing off your extensive knowledge of the answer to the first one.

7) Be attentive

You only have 20 minutes or so, and you should keep your attention at its sharpest throughout. When a member is addressing a problem or question to you, give him your undivided attention. Address your reply principally to him, but do not exclude the other board members.

8) Do not interrupt

A board member may be stating a problem for you to analyze. He will ask you a question when the time comes. Let him state the problem, and wait for the question.

9) Make sure you understand the question

Do not try to answer until you are sure what the question is. If it is not clear, restate it in your own words or ask the board member to clarify it for you. However, do not haggle about minor elements.

10) Reply promptly but not hastily

A common entry on oral board rating sheets is "candidate responded readily," or "candidate hesitated in replies." Respond as promptly and quickly as you can, but do not jump to a hasty, ill-considered answer.

11) Do not be peremptory in your answers

A brief answer is proper – but do not fire your answer back. That is a losing game from your point of view. The board member can probably ask questions much faster than you can answer them.

12) Do not try to create the answer you think the board member wants

He is interested in what kind of mind you have and how it works – not in playing games. Furthermore, he can usually spot this practice and will actually grade you down on it.

13) Do not switch sides in your reply merely to agree with a board member

Frequently, a member will take a contrary position merely to draw you out and to see if you are willing and able to defend your point of view. Do not start a debate, yet do not surrender a good position. If a position is worth taking, it is worth defending.

14) Do not be afraid to admit an error in judgment if you are shown to be wrong

The board knows that you are forced to reply without any opportunity for careful consideration. Your answer may be demonstrably wrong. If so, admit it and get on with the interview.

15) Do not dwell at length on your present job

The opening question may relate to your present assignment. Answer the question but do not go into an extended discussion. You are being examined for a *new* job, not your present one. As a matter of fact, try to phrase ALL your answers in terms of the job for which you are being examined.

Basis of Rating

Probably you will forget most of these "do's" and "don'ts" when you walk into the oral interview room. Even remembering them all will not ensure you a passing grade. Perhaps you did not have the qualifications in the first place. But remembering them will help you to put your best foot forward, without treading on the toes of the board members.

Rumor and popular opinion to the contrary notwithstanding, an oral board wants you to make the best appearance possible. They know you are under pressure – but they also want to see how you respond to it as a guide to what your reaction would be under the pressures of the job you seek. They will be influenced by the degree of poise you display, the personal traits you show and the manner in which you respond.

ABOUT THIS BOOK

This book contains tests divided into Examination Sections. Go through each test, answering every question in the margin. We have also attached a sample answer sheet at the back of the book that can be removed and used. At the end of each test look at the answer key and check your answers. On the ones you got wrong, look at the right answer choice and learn. Do not fill in the answers first. Do not memorize the questions and answers, but understand the answer and principles involved. On your test, the questions will likely be different from the samples. Questions are changed and new ones added. If you understand these past questions you should have success with any changes that arise. Tests may consist of several types of questions. We have additional books on each subject should more study be advisable or necessary for you. Finally, the more you study, the better prepared you will be. This book is intended to be the last thing you study before you walk into the examination room. Prior study of relevant texts is also recommended. NLC publishes some of these in our Fundamental Series. Knowledge and good sense are important factors in passing your exam. Good luck also helps. So now study this Passbook, absorb the material contained within and take that knowledge into the examination. Then do your best to pass that exam.

EXAMINATION SECTION

EXAMINATION SECTION
TEST 1

Memory for Addresses Test

DIRECTIONS: In this test you will have to memorize the locations (A, B, C, D or E) of 25 addresses shown in five boxes. For example, "Sardis" is in box "C," "4300-4799 West" is in box "E," etc. Study the locations of the addresses for five minutes (try sounding them to yourself), then cover the boxes and try to answer the questions below. *PRINT THE LETTER OF THE CORRECT ANSWER IN THE SPACE AT THE RIGHT.*

Box A	Box B	Box C
4700-5599 Table	6800-6999 Table	5600-6499 Table
Lismore	Kelford	Joel
4800-5199 West	5200-5799 West	3200-3499 West
Hesper	Musella	Sardis
5500-6399 Blake	4800-5499 Blake	6400-7299 Blake

Box D	Box E
6500-6799 Table	4400-4699 Table
Tatum	Ruskin
3500-4299 West	4300-4799 West
Porter	Somers
4300-4799 Blake	7300-7499 Blake

1. Musella   1.____
2. 4300-4799 Blake   2.____
3. 4700-5599 Table   3.____
4. Tatum   4.____
5. 5500-6399 Blake   5.____
6. Hesper   6.____
7. Kelford   7.____
8. Somers   8.____
9. 6400-7299 Blake   9.____
10. Joel   10.____
11. 5500-6399 Blake   11.____
12. 5200-5799 West   12.____
13. Porter   13.____
14. 7300-7499 Blake   14.____

KEY (CORRECT ANSWERS)

1. B
2. D
3. A
4. D
5. A
6. A
7. B
8. E
9. C
10. C
11. A
12. B
13. D
14. E

TEST 2

Address Checking Test

DIRECTIONS: In this test you will have to decide whether two addresses are alike or different. If the two addresses are exactly alike in every way, mark the answer "A." If the two addresses are different, mark the answer "D." *PRINT THE LETTER OF THE CORRECT ANSWER IN THE SPACE AT THE RIGHT.*

1. 2134 S. 20th St.   2134 S. 20th St.   1._____
2. 4608 N. Warnock St.   4806 N. Warnock St.   2._____
3. 1202 W. Girard Dr.   1202 W. Girard Rd.   3._____
4. Chappaqua, NY 10514   Chappaqua, NY 10514   4._____
5. 2207 Markland Ave.   2207 Markham Ave.   5._____

General Test

DIRECTIONS: In this test there are three kinds of questions—Vocabulary, Reading and Number Series. For Vocabulary questions, like number 6, choose the suggested answer that means most nearly the same as the word or words in italics. For Reading questions, like number 7, read the paragraph and answer the question that follows it. For Number Series questions, like numbers 8 through 25, there is a series of numbers which is arranged in some definite order or pattern, followed by five sets of two numbers each. Determine the order or pattern of the numbers at the left and choose from the selections below the two numbers that would properly continue the order or pattern. *PRINT THE LETTER OF THE CORRECT ANSWER IN THE SPACE AT THE RIGHT.*

6. The reports were *consolidated by* the secretary. *Consolidated* most nearly means   6._____

    A. combined   B. concluded   C. distributed   D. protected   E. weighed

7. "Post office clerks assigned to stamp windows are directly responsible financially in the   7._____
   selling of postage. In addition, they are expected to have a thorough knowledge as to the acceptability of matter offered for mailing. Any information which they give out to the public must be accurate."
   The paragraph best supports the statement that clerks assigned to stamp-window duty

    A. must account for stamps issued to them for sale
    B. have had long training in other post-office work
    C. advise the public only on matters of official business
    D. must refer continuously to the sources of postal regulations
    E. inspect the contents of every package offered for mailing

8. 1 2 3 4 5 6 7 ...   8._____

    A. 1 2   B. 5 6   C. 8 9
    D. 4 5   E. 7 8

2 (#2)

9. 15 14 13 12 11 10 9 ...

   A. 2 1
   B. 17 16
   C. 8 9
   D. 8 7
   E. 9 8

   9.____

10. 20 20 21 21 22 22 23 ...

    A. 23 23
    B. 23 24
    C. 19 19
    D. 22 23
    E. 21 22

    10.____

11. 17 3 17 4 17 5 17 ...

    A. 6 17
    B. 6 7
    C. 17 6
    D. 5 6
    E. 17 7

    11.____

12. 1 2 4 5 7 8 10 ...

    A. 11 12
    B. 12 14
    C. 10 13
    D. 12 13
    E. 11 13

    12.____

13. 21 21 20 20 19 19 18 ...

    A. 18 18
    B. 18 17
    C. 17 18
    D. 17 17
    E. 18 19

    13.____

14. 1 22 1 23 1 24 1 ...

    A. 26 1
    B. 25 26
    C. 25 1
    D. 1 26
    E. 1 25

    14.____

15. 1 20 3 19 5 18 7 ...

    A. 8 9
    B. 8 17
    C. 17 10
    D. 17 9
    E. 9 18

    15.____

16. 4 7 10 13 16 19 22 ...

    A. 23 26
    B. 25 27
    C. 25 26
    D. 25 28
    E. 24 27

    16.____

17. 30 2 28 4 26 6 24 ...

    A. 23 9
    B. 26 8
    C. 8 9
    D. 26 22
    E. 8 22

    17.____

18. 5 6 20 7 8 19 9 ...

    A. 10 18
    B. 18 17
    C. 10 7
    D. 18 19
    E. 10 11

    18.____

19. 9 10 1 11 12 2 13 ...

    A. 2 14
    B. 3 14
    C. 14 3
    D. 14 15
    E. 14 1

    19.____

20. 4 6 9 11 14 16 19 ...

    A. 21 24
    B. 22 25
    C. 20 22
    D. 21 23
    E. 22 24

    20.____

21. 8 8 1 10 10 3 12 ...   21._____

    A. 13 13   B. 12 5   C. 12 4
    D. 13 5   E. 4 12

22. 14 1 2 15 3 4 16...   22._____

    A. 5 16   B. 6 7   C. 5 17
    D. 5 6   E. 17 5

23. 10 12 50 15 17 50 20 ...   23._____

    A. 50 21   B. 21 50   C. 50 22
    D. 22 50   E. 22 24

24. 1 2 3 50 4 5 6 51 7 8...   24._____

    A. 9 10   B. 9 52   C. 51 10
    D. 10 52   E. 10 50

25. 20 21 23 24 27 28 32 33 38 39 ...   25._____

    A. 45 46   B. 45 52   C. 44 45
    D. 44 49   E. 40 46

KEY (CORRECT ANSWERS)

           1. A   11. A
           2. D   12. E
           3. D   13. B
           4. A   14. C
           5. D   15. D

           6. A   16. D
           7. A   17. E
           8. C   18. A
           9. D   19. C
          10. B   20. A

                     21. B
                     22. D
                     23. D
                     24. B
                     25. A

Address Checking

DESCRIPTION OF THE TEST AND SAMPLE QUESTIONS

Every member of the Postal work force is responsible for seeing that every letter reaches the right address. If one worker makes an error in reading an address, it can cause a serious delay in getting the letter to where it is supposed to go.

Both the Clerk-Carrier and Mail Handler examinations include tests of address checking. The test in the Clerk-Carrier examination is harder than the one in the Mail Handler examination. The Mail Handler test has only names of cities and states with some zip codes, while the Clerk-Carrier test has street addresses also.

Can you spot whether or not two addresses are alike or different? It is as easy as that. But how fast can you do it accurately? Look at the sample questions below. Each question consists of a pair of addresses like this—

762 W 18th St   762 W 18th St
    Are they Alike or Different? They are exactly Alike.
9486 Hillsdale Rd   9489 Hillsdale Rd
    Alike or Different? They are Different. Do you see why?
1242 RegalSt   1242 Regel St
    Alike or Different?

Remember that this test measures both speed and accuracy. So work as fast as you can without making any mistakes. Have a friend time you while you are working on the practice tests—you may find that you get faster as you become used to this type of question.

Hints for Answering Address-Checking Questions
- Do not spend too much time on any one question.
- The difference may not be noticeable at first, so be sure to check
  —all numbers (are they alike and in the same order or are they different)
  —abbreviations, such as St, Rd, NW, N Y (are they alike or are they different)
  —spellings of street, city, and state names
- Do not get nervous about the time limit. (In the official test no one is expected to do all the questions in the time allowed.)
- Make sure that you have marked the correct box for each question.

Address Checking—Sample Questions

Starting now, if the two addresses are ALIKE darken box A on the Sample Answer Sheet below. If the two addresses are DIFFERENT in any way darken box D. Answer every question.

1 ... 239 Windell Ave   239 Windell Ave
   Alike or Different? Alike. Mark space A for question 1.
2 ... 4667 Edgeworth Rd   4677 Edgeworth Rd
   Alike or Different? Different. Mark space D for question 2.
3 ... 2661 Kennel St SE   2661 Kennel St SW
4 ... 3709 Columbine St   3707 Columbine St
5 ... 969 W 14th St NW   969 W 14th St NW
6 ... 4439 Frederick Pkwy   4439 Frederick Pkwy
7 ... 77 Summers St   77 Summers St
8 ... 828 N Franklin Pl   828 S Franklin Pl

Check your answers with the correct answers. If you have any wrong answers, be sure you see why before you go on.

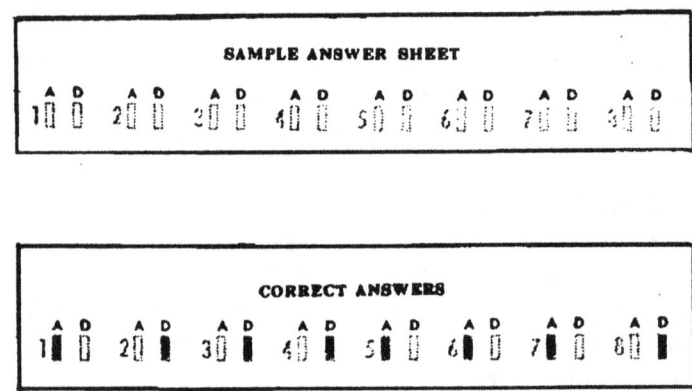

The addresses in the Practice Tests are like the ones you will have to check in the examinations. The ones in Practice Test 1 are like the ones in the Mail Handler examination. Work as fast as you can, but be careful because you will lose points for making mistakes. Be sure to take no more than the correct time for each test. Check your answers with the answers at the end of each test.

Now turn the page and take the first Practice Test.

ADDRESS CHECKING—PRACTICE TEST 1

Work exactly *3 minutes*. No more. No less. If you finish before the 3 minutes are up, go over your answers again. Be sure to mark your answers on the Sample Answer Sheet on the next page.

1 ...	Purdin Mo	Purdon Mo
2 ...	Hobart Ind 46342	Hobart Ind 46342
3 ...	Kuna Idaho	Kuna Idaho
4 ...	Janesville Calif 96114	Janesville Calif 96119
5 ...	Sioux Falls S Dak	Sioux Falls S Dak
6 ...	Homewood Miss	Homewood Miss
7 ...	Kaweah Calif	Kawaeh Calif
8 ...	Unionport Ohio	Unionport Ohio
9 ...	Meyersdale Pa	Meyersdale Va
10 ...	Coquille Oreg 97423	Coqville Oreg 97423
11 ...	Milan Wis	Milam Wis
12 ...	Prospect Ky	Prospect Ky
13 ...	Cloversville N Y	Cloverville N Y
14 ...	Locate Mont 59340	Locate Mont 59340
15 ...	Bozman Md	Bozeman Md
16 ...	Orient Ill	Orient Ill
17 ...	Yosemite Ky 42566	Yosemite Ky 42566
18 ...	Camden Miss 39045	Camden Miss 39054
19 ...	Bennington Vt	Bennington Vt
20 ...	La Farge Wis	La Farge Wis
21 ...	Fairfield N Y	Fairfield N C
22 ...	Wynot Nebr	Wynot Nebr
23 ...	Arona Pa	Aroda Pa
24 ...	Thurman N C 28683	Thurmond N C 28683
25 ...	Zenda Kans	Zenba Kans
26 ...	Pike N H	Pike N H
27 ...	Gorst Wash 98337	Gorst Wash 98837
28 ...	Joiner Ark	Joiner Ark
29 ...	Normangee Tex	Normangee Tex
30 ...	Toccoa Ga	Tococa Ga
31 ...	Small Point Maine 04567	Small Point Maine 04567
32 ...	Eagan Tenn	Eagar Tenn
33 ...	Belfield N Dak	Belford N Dak
34 ...	De Ridder La 70634	De Ridder La 70634
35 ...	Van Meter Iowa	Van Meter Iowa
36 ...	Valparaiso Fla	Valparaiso Ind
37 ...	Souris N Dak	Souris N Dak
38 ...	Robbinston Maine	Robbinstown Maine
39 ...	Dawes W Va 25054	Dawes W Va 25054
40 ...	Goltry Okla	Goltrey Okla

[Sample Answer Sheet and Correct Answers grids for Part A, items 1–40]

Now check your answers by comparing your answers with the correct answers shown below.

Count how many you got right, and write that number on this line ──────────────▶ Number Right ─────

Now count how many you got wrong, and write that number on this line ──────────────▶ Number Wrong =====

Subtract the Number Wrong from the Number Right and write the Difference on this line ──────────────▶ Total Score ─────

Meaning of Test Score
    If your Total Score is *26 or more,* you have a Good score.
    If your Total Score is from *16 to 25,* you have a Fair score.
    If your Total Score is *15 or less,* you are not doing too well.
        You may be going too slowly, or you may be making too many mistakes. You need more practice.

ADDRESS CHECKING—PRACTICE TEST 2

These addresses are a little harder.

Remember to work as fast as you can but be careful. Work exactly *3 minutes.* No more. No less. If you finish before the 3 minutes are up, go over your answers again. Be sure to mark your answers on the Sample Answer Sheet on the next page.

1 ...	7961 Eastern Ave SE	7961 Eastern Ave SE
2 ...	3809 20th Rd N	3309 20th Rd N
3 ...	Smicksburg Pa	Smithsburg Pa
4 ...	Sherman Conn	Sherman Conn
5 ...	Richland Ga	Richland La
6 ...	8520 Leesburg Pike SE	8520 Leesburg Pike SE
7 ...	Genevia Ark	Geneva Ark
8 ...	104 W Jefferson St	104 W Jefferson St
9 ...	Meandor WVa	Meander W Va
10 ...	6327 W Mari Ct	6327 W Mari Ct
11 ...	3191 Draper Dr SE	3191 Draper Dr SW
12 ...	1415 W Green Spring Rd	1415 W Green Spring Rd
13 ...	Parr Ind	Parr Ind
14 ...	East Falmouth Mass 02536	East Falmouth Miss 02536
15 ...	3016 N St NW	3016 M St NW
16 ...	Yukon Mo	Yukon Mo
17 ...	7057 Brookfield Plaza	7057 Brookfield Plaza
18 ...	Bethel Ohio 45106	Bethel Ohio 45106
19 ...	Littleton N H	Littleton N C
20 ...	8909 Bowie Dr	8909 Bowie Dr
21 ...	Colmar I11	Colmar I11
22 ...	784 Matthews Dr NE	784 Matthews Dr NE
23 ...	2923 John Marshall Dr	2932 John Marshall Dr
24 ...	6023 Woodmont Rd	6023 Woodmount Rd
25 ...	Nolan Tex	Noland Tex
26 ...	342 E Lincolnia Rd	342 E Lincolnia Dr
27 ...	Jane Calif	Jane Calif
28 ...	4921 Seminary Rd	4912 Seminary Rd
29 ...	Ulmers S C	Ullmers S C
30 ...	4804 Montgomery Lane SW	4804 Montgomery Lane SW
31 ...	210 E Fairfax Dr	210 W Fairfax Dr
32 ...	Hanapepe Hawaii	Hanapepe Hawaii
33 ...	450 La Calle del Punto	450 La Calle del Punto
34 ...	Walland Tenn 37886	Walland Tenn 37836
35 ...	Villamont Va	Villamont Va
36 ...	4102 Georgia Ave NW	4102 Georgia Rd NW
37 ...	Aroch Oreg	Aroch Oreg
38 ...	6531 N Walton Ave	6531 N Waldon Ave
39 ...	Jeff Ky	Jeff Ky
40 ...	Delphos Iowa	Delphis Iowa

SAMPLE ANSWER SHEET

PART A: [answer bubbles numbered 1–40, A/D options]

Now check your answers by comparing your answers with the correct answers shown below.

CORRECT ANSWERS

PART A: [answer bubbles numbered 1–40, A/D options with correct answers marked]

Count how many you got right, and write that number on this line ──────────────▶ Number Right _____

Now count how many you got wrong, and write that number on this line ──────────────▶ Number Wrong _____

Subtract the Number Wrong from the Number Right and write the Difference on this line ──────────────▶ Total Score _____

Meaning of Test Score

If your Total Score is *26 or more,* you have a Good score.

If your Total Score is from *16 to 25,* you have a Fair score.

If your Total Score is *15 or less,* you are not doing too well.

You may be going too slowly, or you may be making too many mistakes. You need more practice.

ADDRESS CHECKING-PRACTICE TEST 3

These addresses are exactly like the ones in the Clerk-Carrier examination. Even if you don't plan to take the Clerk-Carrier examination, this is good practice for the Mail Handler one. Work as fast as you can without making too many errors. Work exactly *3 minutes*. No more. No less. If you finish before the 3 minutes are up, go over your answers again. Mark your answers on the Sample Answer Sheet on the next page.

1 ...	2134 S 20th St	2134 S 20th St
2 ...	4608 N Warnock St	4806 N Warnock St
3 ...	1202 W Girard Dr	1202 W Girard Rd
4 ...	3120 S Harcourt St	3120 S Harcourt St
5 ...	4618 W Addison St	4618 E Addison St
6 ...	Sessums Miss	Sessoms Miss
7 ...	6425 N Delancey	6425 N Delancey
8 ...	5407 Columbia Rd	5407 Columbia Rd
9 ...	2106 Southern Ave	2106 Southern Ave
10 ...	Highfalls N C 27259	Highlands NC 27259
11 ...	2873 Pershing Dr	2873 Pershing Dr
12 ...	1329 N H Ave NW	1329 N J Ave NW
13 ...	1316 N Quinn St	1316 N Quinn St
14 ...	7507 Wyngate Dr	7505 Wyngate Dr
15 ...	2918 Colesville Rd	2918 Colesvale Rd
16 ...	2071 E Belvedere Dr	2071 E Belvedere Dr
17 ...	Palmer Wash	Palmer Mich
18 ...	2106 16th St SW	2106 16th St SW
19 ...	2207 Markland Ave	2207 Markham Ave
20 ...	5345 16th St SW	5345 16th St SE
21 ...	239 Summit Pl NE	239 Summit Pl NE
22 ...	152 Continental Pkwy	152 Continental Blvd
23 ...	8092 13th Rd S	8029 13th Rd S
24 ...	3906 Queensbury Rd	3906 Queensbury Rd
25 ...	4719 Linnean Ave NW	4719 Linnean Ave NE
26 ...	Bradford Me	Bradley Me
27 ...	Parrott Ga 31777	Parrott Ga 31177
28 ...	4312 Lowell Lane	4312 Lowell Lane
29 ...	6929 W 135th Place	6929 W 135th Plaza
30 ...	5143 Somerset Cir	5143 Somerset Cir
31 ...	8501 Kennedy St	8501 Kennedy St
32 ...	2164 E McLean Ave	2164 E McLean Ave
33 ...	7186 E St NW	7186 F St NW
34 ...	2121 Beechcrest Rd	2121 Beechcroft Rd
35 ...	3609 E Montrose St	3609 E Montrose St
36 ...	324 S Alvadero St	324 S Alverado St
37 ...	2908 Plaza de las Estrellas	2908 Plaza de las Estrellas
38 ...	223 Great Falls Rd SE	223 Great Falls Dr SE
39 ...	Kelton S C 29354	Kelton S C 29354
40 ...	3201 Landover Rd	3201 Landover Rd

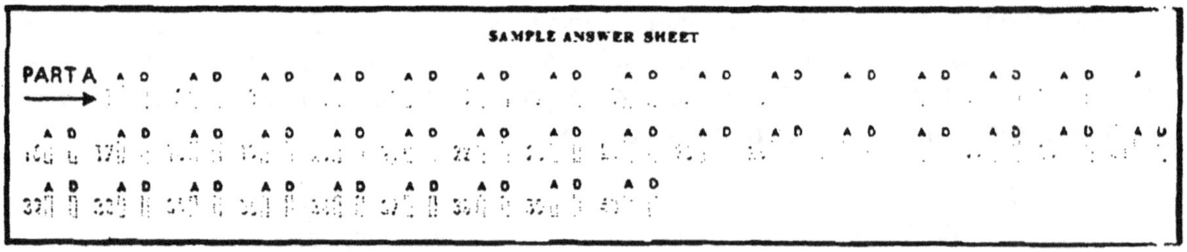

[SAMPLE ANSWER SHEET grid]

Now check your answers by comparing your answers with the correct answers shown below.

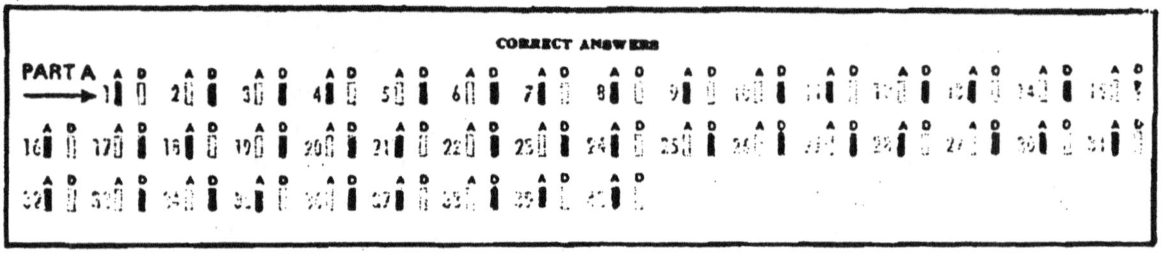

[CORRECT ANSWERS grid]

Count how many you got right, and write that number on this line ————————————————▶ Number Right ———

Now count how many you got wrong, and write that number on this line ————————————————▶ Number Wrong ———

Subtract the Number Wrong from the Number Right and write the Difference on this line ———————▶ Total Score ———

Meaning of Test Score.
    If your Total Score is *26 or more,* you have a Good score.
    If your Total Score is from *16 to 25,* you have a Fair score.
    If your Total Score is *15 or less,* you are not doing too well.
        You may be going too slowly, or you may be making too many mistakes. You need more practice.

ADDRESS CHECKING

EXAMINATION SECTION
TEST 1

DIRECTIONS: This test is designed to measure your speed and accuracy. You are urged to work both quickly and accurately and to do correctly as many lists as you can in the time allowed. The test consists of lists of pairs of addresses. Circle the letter A on your answer sheet if the two addresses are exactly ALIKE in every way. Circle the letter D if they are DIFFERENT.

CIRCLE CORRECT ANSWER

1.	2134 S 20th St	2134 S 20th St	A	D
2.	4608 N Warnock St	4806 N Warnock St	A	D
3.	1202 W Girard Dr	1202 W Girard Rd	A	D
4.	3120 S Harcourt St	3120 S Harcourt St	A	D
5.	4618 W Addison St	4618 E Addison St	A	D
6.	39-B Parkway Rd	39-D Parkway Rd	A	D
7.	6425 N Delancey	6425 N Delancey	A	D
8.	5407 Columbia Rd	5407 Columbia Rd	A	D
9.	2106 Southern Ave	2106 Southern Ave	A	D
10.	Highfalls NC	Highlands NC	A	D
11.	2873 Pershing Dr	2673 Pershing Dr	A	D
12.	1329 N H Ave NW	1329 N J Ave NW	A	D
13.	13 1316 N Quinn St Arl	1316 N Quinn St Alex	A	D
14.	7507 Wyngate Dr	7505 Wyngate Dr	A	D
15.	15 2918 Colesville Rd	2918 Colesville Rd	A	D
16.	16 2071 Belvedere Dr	2071 Belvedere Dr	A	D
17.	Palmer Wash	Palmer Mich	A	D
18.	2106 16th St SW	2106 16th St SW	A	D
19.	64-23 229th St	64-23 229th St	A	D
20.	8744 E St NE	8744 E St NE	A	D
21.	668-15 Lee Dr	668-151 Lee Dr	A	D
22.	84-84 Bay 16 St	84-84 Baye 16 St	A	D
23.	1117 E Egg Lane	11117 E Egg Lane	A	D
24.	36 W Pingrey Dr Easterville Md	36 W Pingrey Dr Easterville Md	A	D
25.	A-34 N 176 Rd NE Doddsville Mich	A-34 N 176 Rd NE Doddsville Mich	A	D

KEY (CORRECT ANSWERS)

1.	A	11.	D
2.	D	12.	D
3.	D	13.	D
4.	A	14.	D
5.	D	15.	A
6.	D	16.	A
7.	A	17.	D
8.	A	18.	A
9.	A	19.	A
10.	D	20.	A

21. D
22. D
23. D
24. A
25. A

———

TEST 2

DIRECTIONS: This test is designed to measure your speed and accuracy. You are urged to work both quickly and accurately and to do correctly as many lists as you can in the time allowed. The test consists of lists of pairs of addresses. Circle the letter *A* on your answer sheet if the two addresses are exactly ALIKE in every way. Circle the letter *D* if they are DIFFERENT.

CIRCLE CORRECT ANSWER

1. 89 Mohicn Pk Ave — 89 Mohcn Pk Ave — A D
2. 355 Warburton Av — 355 Waburton Av — A D
3. 20 Otis Ave — 20 Otis Av — A D
4. Tuttle Dr Osning — Tuttle Dr Osning — A D
5. 15 South Pl Chapqa — 15 South Pl Chapqua — A D
6. 83 McLean Ave — 83 McLean Av — A D
7. 168 Ellison Ave Bronxvil — 168 Ellson Av Bronxvil — A D
8. 77 Lvngstn Av — 79 Lvngstn Ave — A D
9. 52 1/2 Wstmnstr Dr — 52 1/2 Wstmnstr Av — A D
10. 10 132A Old Crompnd Rd — 132A Old Crompond Rd — A D
11. 581 Bway Hastgs-on-Hdsn — 581 Bway Hstg-on-Hdson — A D
12. 682 Scrsdl Rd NW — 682 Scrsdl Rd NW — A D
13. 109 S Regent Mt Ksco — 109 S Regent Mt.Ksco — A D
14. 151 N Frnch Ave Elmsfrd — 151 N Frnch Ave Elmfrd — A D
15. 12 Gomer Jefrsn Vly — 12 Gomar Jefrsn Vly — A D
16. 391 Plesnt Nw Roch — 391 Plesnt NW Roch — A D
17. 22 1/2A Keogh La — 22 1/2A Keoh La — A D
18. 159 Meetg Hse Rd Bdfrd — 15 Meetg Hse Rd Bdfrd — A D
19. 2131 Shrad Rd Brirclf Mnr — 2131 Shrd Rd Brirclf Mnr — A D
20. 139 Amackasn Ter SE — 139 Amckasn Ter SE — A D

KEY (CORRECT ANSWERS)

1.	D	11.	D
2.	D	12.	A
3.	D	13.	D
4.	D	14.	D
5.	D	15.	D
6.	D	16.	D
7.	D	17.	D
8.	D	18.	D
9.	D	19.	D
10.	D	20.	D

TEST 3

DIRECTIONS: This test is designed to measure your speed and accuracy. You are urged to work both quickly and accurately and to do correctly as many lists as you can in the time allowed. The test consists of lists of pairs of addresses. Circle the letter *A* on your answer sheet if the two addresses are exactly ALIKE in every way. Circle the letter *D* if they are DIFFERENT.

			CIRCLE CORRECT ANSWER	
1.	429 Nthn Hale Dr Hntgtn	429 Nthn Hale Dr Htgtn	A	D
2.	111 Shubrt Dr Haupaug	111 Shubrt Dr Haupaug	A	D
3.	156 Somrs La&Indn Hd Rd	167 Somers La & Indn Hd Rd	A	D
4.	1996 Sunst Av Wsthmptn Bch	199 Sunst Av Wsthmptn Bch	A	D
5.	135 W Shincok Rd Quog	135 W Shinck Rd Quog	A	D
6.	1579 B Strght Pth Wyandnch	1579B Strght Pth Wyandich	A	D
7.	1056 Yoakm Av	1056 Yoakum Av	A	D
8.	59 Wohsepe Dr Brghtwtrs	59 Wohsepe Dr Brghtwtrs	A	D
9.	1131A Wlt Whtmn Rd	1131 Wh Whtmn Rd	A	D
10.	137 Conscnce Cir Setukt	137 Consnce Cir Setukt	A	D
11.	941 Duane Dr Lk Rnknkma	941 Duanne Dr Lk Rnknkma	A	D
12.	1896 Hustn Lndnhrst	1896 Hustn Lndnhrst	A	D
13.	187 E Islip Rd W Islip	187 E Islip Rd Islip	A	D
14.	51 Blugras La	51 Bluegras La	A	D
15.	1B Bodtch Pth Cntr Mrich	1B Bodtch Pth Centr Mrich	A	D
16.	158 Grist Ml La Halsite	158 Grist Ml La Hallsite	A	D
17.	161-35 Shendoa Blvd	161-35 Shenendoa Blvd	A	D
18.	11 Mt Sinai-Coram Rd	11 Mt Sinai-Coram Rd	A	D
19.	31-1B Old Northprt Rd & Kngs Pk Rd	31-1B Old Northprt Rd & Kngs Pk Rd	A	D
20.	867 Medfrd Ave	869 Medfrd Ave	A	D

KEY (CORRECT ANSWERS)

1. D
2. A
3. D
4. D
5. D

6. D
7. D
8. A
9. D
10. D

11. D
12. A
13. D
14. D
15. D

16. D
17. D
18. A
19. A
20. D

TEST 4

DIRECTIONS: This test is designed to measure your speed and accuracy. You are urged to work both quickly and accurately and to do correctly as many lists as you can in the time allowed. The test consists of lists of pairs of addresses. Circle the letter *A* on your answer sheet if the two addresses are exactly ALIKE in every way. Circle the letter *D* if they are DIFFERENT.

CIRCLE CORRECT ANSWER

1.	2469 Dogwd Av E Medo	2467 Dogwd Av E Medo	A	D
2.	5613 Lakevw Av Rkvl Cntr	5613 Lakevw Av Rkv Cntr	A	D
3.	481 Shlbrn La Nw Hyd Pk	481 Shlbrn La Nw Hyd Pk	A	D
4.	246 Court Ocnsde	246 Cort Ocnsde	A	D
5.	437 Juneau Blvd Wdbry	437 Junaeu Blvd Wdbry	A	D
6.	376 Wood La Levitwn	376 Wood La Levitwn	A	D
7.	69 Aspn Flrl Pk	59 Aspn Flr Pk	A	D
8.	2835 Vilag La N Wntagh	2835 Vilage La N Wntagh	A	D
9.	3109 Devnshr Dr E Nrwch	3109 Devnshr Dr E Nrwch	A	D
10.	81-64 Yung Pl Wdmr	81-64 Young Pl Wdmr	A	D
11.	84C Muirfld Rd	84C Muirfld Rd	A	D
12.	23 Bamboola Hksvl	23 Bamboola Hksvl	A	D
13.	139D Pninsla Blvd Vly Strm	139 Pninsla Blvd Vly Strm	A	D
14.	187 Wdland Dr Plandom	187 Wdlan Dr Plandom	A	D
15.	3 Renvil Ct Mil Nk	3 Renvil Ct Ml Nk	A	D
16.	619 Cresnt Dr Old Bthpg	619 Crescnt Dr Old Bthpg	A	D
17.	1518 Unqua Rd Maspeqa	1518 Uniqua Rd Maspeqa	A	D
18.	1017 Renselr Av Atl Bch	1017 Renselr Av Atl Bch	A	D
19.	777 Brook Ct N Nw Hyd Pk	777 Brook Ct Nw Hyd Pk	A	D
20.	2016 Revre Rd Rslyn Hts	2016 Revre Rd Rsyln Hts	A	D

KEY (CORRECT ANSWERS)

1. D
2. D
3. A
4. D
5. D

6. A
7. D
8. D
9. A
10. D

11. A
12. A
13. D
14. D
15. D

16. D
17. D
18. A
19. D
20. D

TEST 5

DIRECTIONS: This test is designed to measure your speed and accuracy. You are urged to work both quickly and accurately and to do correctly as many lists as you can in the time allowed. The test consists of lists of pairs of addresses. Circle the letter A on your answer sheet if the two addresses are exactly ALIKE in every way. Circle the letter D if they are DIFFERENT.

			CIRCLE CORRECT ANSWER	
1.	2512 Pascack Rd Prms	2512 Pasack Rd Prms	A	D
2.	157 Wdlnd Dr Wdclf Lk	157 Wdlnd Dr Wdclf Lk	A	D
3.	2416A Andrsn Blvd Bgfd	2416 Andrsn Av Bgfd	A	D
4.	6215 Athlone Ter Rivr Vl	6215 Athlone Ter Rvr Vl	A	D
5.	666 Plsnt Av Up Sadl Riv	666 Plst Av Up Sadl Riv	A	D
6.	999 Elliott Pl Ruth	999 Eliott Pl Ruth	A	D
7.	357 Blauvlt Dr Hrngtn Pk	357 Blauvlt Dr Hrngtn Pk	A	D
8.	61-34 Upland Rd Ramsy	61-34 Upland Rd Rumsy	A	D
9.	1793 Arcadn Wy Plsd	179 Arcadn Wy Plsd	A	D
10.	3117 Lantna Av Engwd	3117 Lantna Av Englwd	A	D
11.	675 Spindler Ter Sd Bk	675 Spindler Ter Sd Bk	A	D
12.	546 Riverview Pl Mahwah	546 Riverview Pl Mawah	A	D
13.	3061 Hack Crist	3061 Hack Crist	A	D
14.	2099 Lemoin Ave Ft Lee	2099 Lamoin Av Ft Lee	A	D
15.	1133 Mnache Av Mmache	1133 Mnache Av Mnanche	A	D
16.	7100 Qn Ann Rd Tea	7100 Qn Ann Rd Tee	A	D
17.	1255 Euclid Ave Rdgfld Pk	1255 Euclid Av Rdgfld Pk	A	D
18.	8013 Godwin Pl Creskl	8031 Godwin Pl Creskl	A	D
19.	38-03A Alwd Pl Fr Ln	38-03A Alwd Pl Fr Ln	A	D
20.	536 Wilkes La Dmnt	536 Willkes La Dmnt	A	D

KEY (CORRECT ANSWERS)

1. D
2. A
3. D
4. D
5. D

6. D
7. A
8. D
9. D
10. D

11. A
12. D
13. A
14. D
15. D

16. D
17. D
18. D
19. A
20. D

———

TEST 6

DIRECTIONS: This test is designed to measure your speed and accuracy. You are urged to work both quickly and accurately and to do correctly as many lists as you can in the time allowed. The test consists of lists of pairs of addresses. Circle the letter *A* on your answer sheet if the two addresses are exactly ALIKE in every way. Circle the letter *D* if they are DIFFERENT.

CIRCLE
CORRECT ANSWER

1.	7961 Eastern Ave SE	7961 Eastern Ave SE	A D
2.	3809 20th Rd N	3309 20th Rd N	A D
3.	Smicksburg Pa	Smithsburg Pa	A D
4.	Sherman Ct	Sherman Ct	A D
5.	Richland Ga	Richland La	A D
6.	8520 Leesburg Pike SE	8520 Leesburg Pike SE	A D
7.	Genevia Ar	Geneva Ar	A D
8.	104 W Jefferson St	104 W Jefferson St	A D
9.	Meandor WV	Meander WV	A D
10.	6327 W Mari Ct	6327 W Mari Ct	A D
11.	3191 Draper Dr SE	3191 Draper Dr SW	A D
12.	1415 W Green Spring Rd	1415 W Green Spring Rd	A D
13.	Parr In	Parr In	A D
14.	East Falmouth Ma 02536	East Falmouth Ms 02536	A D
15.	3016 N St NW	3015 M St NW	A D
16.	Yukon Mo	Yukon Mo	A D
17.	7057 Brookfield Plaza	7057 Brookfield Plaza	A D
18.	Bethel Oh 45106	Bethel Oh 45106	A D
19.	Littleton NH	Littleton NC	A D
20.	8909 Bowie Dr	8909 Bowie Dr	A D

KEY (CORRECT ANSWERS)

1. A
2. D
3. D
4. A
5. D

6. A
7. D
8. A
9. D
10. A

11. D
12. A
13. A
14. D
15. D

16. A
17. A
18. A
19. D
20. A

TEST 7

DIRECTIONS: This test is designed to measure your speed and accuracy. You are urged to work both quickly and accurately and to do correctly as many lists as you can in the time allowed. The test consists of lists of pairs of addresses. Circle the letter *A* on your answer sheet if the two addresses are exactly ALIKE in every way. Circle the letter *D* if they are DIFFERENT.

CIRCLE CORRECT ANSWER

1. Colmar Il — Colmar Il — A D
2. 784 Matthews Dr NE — 784 Matthews Dr NE — A D
3. 2923 John Marshall Dr — 2932 John Marshall Dr — A D
4. 6023 Woodmont Rd — 6023 Woodmount Rd — A D
5. Nolan Tx — Noland Tx — A D
6. 342 E Lincolnia Rd — 342 E Lincolnia Dr — A D
7. Jane Ca — Jane Ca — A D
8. 4921 Seminary Rd — 4912 Seminary Rd — A D
9. Ulmers SC — Ullmers SC — A D
10. 4804 Montgomery Lane SW — 48-64 Montgomery Lane SW — A D
11. 210 E Fairfax Dr — 210 W Pairfax Dr — A D
12. Hanapepe Hi — Hanapepe Hi — A D
13. 450 La Calle del Punto — 450 La Calle del Punto — A D
14. Walland Tn 37886 — Walland Tn 37836 — A D
15. Villamont Va — Villamont Va — A D
16. 4102 Georgia Ave NW — 4102 Georgia Rd NW — A D
17. Aroch Or — Aroch Or — A D
18. 6531 N Walton Ave — 6531 N Waldon Ave — A D
19. Jeff Ky — Jeff Ky — A D
20. Delphos Ia — Delphis Ia — A D

KEY (CORRECT ANSWERS)

1.	A	11.	D
2.	A	12.	A
3.	D	13.	A
4.	D	14.	D
5.	D	15.	A
6.	D	16.	D
7.	A	17.	A
8.	D	18.	D
9.	D	19.	A
10.	A	20.	D

ADDRESS CHECKING

EXAMINATION SECTION
TEST 1

DIRECTIONS: This test is designed to measure your speed and accuracy. You are urged to work both quickly and accurately and to do correctly as many lists as you can in the time allowed. The test consists of lists of pairs of addresses. Circle the letter *A* on your answer sheet if the two addresses are exactly ALIKE in every way. Circle the letter *D* if they are DIFFERENT.

CIRCLE CORRECT ANSWER

1.	405 Winter Rd NW	405 Winter Rd NW	A	D
2.	607 S Calaveras Rd	607 S Calaveras Rd	A	D
3.	8406 La Casa St	8406 La Cosa St	A	D
4.	121 N Rippon St	121 N Rippon St	A	D
5.	Wideman Ar	Wiseman Ar	A	D
6.	Sodus NY 14551	Sodus NY 14551	A	D
7.	3429 Hermosa Dr	3429 Hermoso Dr	A	D
8.	3628 S Zeeland St	3268 S Zeeland St	A	D
9.	1330 Cheverly Ave NE	1330 Cheverly Ave NE	A	D
10.	1689 N Derwood Dr	1689 N Derwood Dr	A	D
11.	3886 Sunrise Ct	3886 Sunrise Ct	A	D
12.	635 La Calle Mayor	653 La Calle Mayor	A	D
13.	2560 Lansford Pl	2560 Lansford St	A	D
14.	4631 Central Ave	4631 Central Ave	A	D
15.	Mason City Ia 50401	Mason City Ia 50401	A	D
16.	758 Los Arboles Ave SE	758 Los Arboles Ave SW	A	D
17.	3282 E Downington St	3282 E Dunnington St	A	D
18.	7117 N Burlingham Ave	7117 N Burlingham Ave	A	D
19.	32 Oaklawn Blvd	32 Oakland Blvd	A	D
20.	1274 Manzana Rd	1274 Manzana Rd	A	D

KEY (CORRECT ANSWERS)

1. A	6. A	11. A	16. D
2. A	7. D	12. D	17. D
3. D	8. D	13. D	18. A
4. A	9. A	14. A	19. D
5. D	10. A	15. A	20. A

TEST 2

DIRECTIONS: This test is designed to measure your speed and accuracy. You are urged to work both quickly and accurately and to do correctly as many lists as you can in the time allowed. The test consists of lists of pairs of addresses. Circle the letter *A* on your answer sheet if the two addresses are exactly ALIKE in every way. Circle the letter *D* if they are DIFFERENT.

			CIRCLE CORRECT ANSWER	
1.	4598 E Kenilworth Dr	4598 E Kenilworth Dr	A	D
2.	Dayton Ok 73449	Dagton Ok 73449	A	D
3.	1172 W 83rd Ave	1127 W 83rd Ave	A	D
4.	6434 E Pulaski St	6434 E Pulaski Ct	A	D
5.	2764 N Rutherford Pl	2764 N Rutherford Pl	A	D
6.	565 Greenville Blvd SW	565 Greenview Blvd SE	A	D
7.	3824 Massasoit St	3824 Massasoit St	A	D
8.	22 Sagnaw Pkwy	22 Saganaw Pkwy	A	D
9.	Byram Ct 10573	Byram Ct 10573	A	D
10.	1928 S Fairfield Ave	1928 S Fairfield St	A	D
11.	36218 Overhills Dr	36218 Overhills Dr	A	D
13.	516 Avenida de Las Americas NW	516 Avenida de Las Americas NW	A	D
14.	7526 Naraganset Pl SW	7526 Naraganset Pl SW	A	D
15.	52626 W Ogelsby Dr	52626 W Ogelsby Dr	A	D
16.	1003 Winchester Rd	1003 Westchester Rd	A	D
17.	3478 W Cavanaugh Ct	3478 W Cavenaugh Ct	A	D
18.	Kendall Ca 90551	Kendell Ca 90551	A	D
19.	225 El Camino Blvd	225 El Camino Av	A	D
20.	7310 Via de los Pisos	7310 Via de los Pinos	A	D

KEY (CORRECT ANSWERS)

1.	A	6.	D	11.	D	16.	D
2.	D	7.	D	12.	A	17.	D
3.	D	8.	A	13.	A	18.	D
4.	D	9.	D	14.	A	19.	D
5.	A	10.	A	15.	A	20.	D

TEST 3

DIRECTIONS: This test is designed to measure your speed and accuracy. You are urged to work both quickly and accurately and to do correctly as many lists as you can in the time allowed. The test consists of lists of pairs of addresses. Circle the letter *A* on your answer sheet if the two addresses are exactly ALIKE in every way. Circle the letter *D* if they are DIFFERENT.

CIRCLE CORRECT ANSWER

1.	1987 Wellington Ave SW	1987 Wellington Ave SW	A	D
2.	3124 S 71st St	3142 S 71st St	A	D
3.	729 Lincolnwood Blvd	729 Lincolnwood Blvd	A	D
4.	1166 N Beaumont Dr	1166 S Beaumont Dr	A	D
5.	3224 W Winecona Pl	3224 W Winecona Pl	A	D
6.	608 La Calle Bienvenida	607 La Calle Bienvenida	A	D
7.	La Molte Ia 52045	La Molte Ia 52045	A	D
8.	8625 Armitage Ave NW	8625 Armitage Ave NW	A	D
9.	2343 Broadview Ave	2334 Broadview Ave	A	D
10.	4279 Sierra Grande -Ave NE	427-9 Sierra Grande Dr NE	A	D
11.	165 32d Ave	165 32d Ave	A	D
12.	12742 N Deerborn St	12724 N Deerborn St	A	D
13.	114 Estancia Ave	141 Estancia Ave	A	D
14.	351 S Berwyn Rd	351 S Berwyn Pl	A	D
15.	7732 Avenida Manana SW	7732 Avenida Manana SW	A	D
16.	6337 C St SW	6337 G St SW	A	D
17.	57895 E Drexyl Ave	58795 E Drexyl Ave	A	D
18.	Altro Tx 75923	Altra Tx 75923	A	D
19.	3465 S Nashville St	3465 N Nashville St	A	D
20.	1226 Odell Blvd NW	1226 Oddell Blvd NW	A	D

KEY (CORRECT ANSWERS)

1. A	6. D	11. A	16. D
2. D	7. A	12. D	17. D
3. A	8. A	13. D	18. D
4. D	9. D	14. D	19. D
5. A	10. D	15. A	20. D

TEST 4

DIRECTIONS: This test is designed to measure your speed and accuracy. You are urged to work both quickly and accurately and to do correctly as many lists as you can in the time allowed. The test consists of lists of pairs of addresses. Circle the letter *A* on your answer sheet if the two addresses are exactly ALIKE in every way. Circle the letter *D* if they are DIFFERENT.

CIRCLE CORRECT ANSWER

1.	94002 Chappel Ct	94002 Chappel Ct	A	D
2.	512 La Vega Dr	512 La Veta Dr	A	D
3.	8774 W Winona Pl	8774 E Winona Pl	A	D
4.	6431 Ingleside St SE	6431 Ingleside St SE	A	D
5.	2270 N Leanington St	2270 N Leanington St	A	D
6.	235 Calle de Los Vecinos	235 Calle de Los Vecinos	A	D
7.	3987 E Westwood Ave	3987 W Westwood Ave	A	D
8.	Skamokawa Wa	Skamohawa Wa	A	D
9.	2674 E Champlain Cir	2764 E Champlain Cir	A	D
10.	8751 Elmhurst Blvd	8751 Elmwood Blvd	A	D
11.	6649 Solano Dr	6649 Solana Dr	A	D
12.	4423 S Escenaba St	4423 S Escenaba St	A	D
13.	1198 N St NW	1198 M St NW	A	D
14.	Sparta Ga	Sparta Va	A	D
15.	96753 Wrightwood Ave	96753 Wrightwood Ave	A	D
16.	2445 Sangamow Ave SE	2445 Sangamow Ave SE	A	D
17.	5117 E 67 Pl	5171 E 67 Pl	A	D
18.	847 Mesa Grande Pl	847 Mesa Grande Ct	A	D
19.	1100 Cermaken St	1100 Cermaker St	A	D
20.	321 Tijeras Ave NW	321 Tijeras Ave NW	A	D

KEY (CORRECT ANSWERS)

1. A	6. A	11. D	16. A
2. D	7. D	12. A	17. D
3. D	8. D	13. D	18. D
4. A	9. D	14. D	19. D
5. A	10. D	15. A	20. A

TEST 5

DIRECTIONS: This test is designed to measure your speed and accuracy. You are urged to work both quickly and accurately and to do correctly as many lists as you can in the time allowed. The test consists of lists of pairs of addresses. Circle the letter *A* on your answer sheet if the two addresses are exactly ALIKE in every way. Circle the letter *D* if they are DIFFERENT.

CIRCLE
CORRECT ANSWER

1.	3405 Prospect St	3405 Prospect St	A	D
2.	6643 Burlington Pl	6643 Burlingtown Pl	A	D
3.	851 Esperanza Blvd	851 Esperanza Blvd	A	D
4.	Jenkinjones WV	Kenkinjones W	A	D
5.	1008 Pennsylvania Ave SE	1008 Pennsylvania Ave SW	A	D
6.	2924 26th St N	2929 26th St N	A	D
7.	7115 Highland Dr	7115 Highland Dr	A	D
8.	Chaptico Md	Chaptica Md	A	D
9.	3508 Camron Mills Rd	3508 Camron Mills Rd	A	D
10.	67158 Capston Dr	67158 Capston Dr	A	D
11.	3613 S Taylor Av	3631 S Taylor Av	A	D
12.	2421 Menokin Dr	2421 Menokin Dr	A	D
13.	3226 M St NW	3226 N St NW	A	D
14.	1201 S Court House Rd	1201 S Court House Rd	A	D
15.	Findlay Ohio 45840	Findley Ohio 45840	A	D
16.	17 Bennett St	17 Bennet St	A	D
17.	7 Vine Bowl Dr	7 Vine Bowl Pl	A	D
18.	126 McKinley Av	126 MacKinley Av	A	D
19.	384 Nepperhan Rd	387 Nepperhan Rd	A	D
20.	1077 Contreras Av NW	1077 Contreras Av NW	A	D

KEY (CORRECT ANSWERS)

1. A
2. D
3. A
4. D
5. D
6. D
7. A
8. D
9. A
10. A
11. D
12. A
13. D
14. A
15. D
16. D
17. D
18. D
19. D
20. A

TEST 6

DIRECTIONS: This test is designed to measure your speed and accuracy. You are urged to work both quickly and accurately and to do correctly as many lists as you can in the time allowed. The test consists of lists of pairs of addresses. Circle the letter *A* on your answer sheet if the two addresses are exactly ALIKE in every way. Circle the letter *D* if they are DIFFERENT.

CIRCLE
CORRECT ANSWER

1.	239 Summit Pl NE	239 Summit Pl NE	A	D
2.	152 Continental Pkwy	152 Continental Blvd	A	D
3.	8092 13th Rd S	8029 13th Rd S	A	D
4.	3906 Queensbury Rd	3906 Queensbury Rd	A	D
5.	4719 Linnean Av NW	4719 Linnean Av NE	A	D
6.	Bradford Me	Bradley Me	A	D
7.	Parrott Ga 31777	Parrott Ga 31177	A	D
8.	4312 Lowell Lane	4312 Lowell Lane	A	D
9.	6929 W 135th Place	6929 W 135th Plaza	A	D
10.	5143 Somerset Cir	5143 Somerset Cir	A	D
11.	8501 Kennedy St	8501 Kennedy St	A	D
12.	2164 E McLean Av	2164 E McLean Av	A	D
13.	7186 E St NW	7186 F St NW	A	D
14.	2121 Beechcrest Rd	2121 Beechcroft Rd	A	D
15.	324 S Alvadero St	324 S Alverado St	A	D
17.	2908 Plaza de las Estrellas	2908 Plaza de las Estrellas	A	D
18.	223 Great Falls Rd SE	223 Great Falls Dr SE	A	D
19.	Kelton SC 29354	Kelton SC 29354	A	D
20.	3201 Landover Rd	3201 Landover Rd	A	D

KEY (CORRECT ANSWERS)

1. A	6. D	11. A	16. D
2. D	7. D	12. A	17. A
3. D	8. A	13. D	18. D
4. A	9. D	14. D	19. A
5. D	10. A	15. A	20. A

TEST 7

DIRECTIONS: This test is designed to measure your speed and accuracy. You are urged to work both quickly and accurately and to do correctly as many lists as you can in the time allowed. The test consists of lists of pairs of addresses. Circle the letter *A* on your answer sheet if the two addresses are exactly ALIKE in every way. Circle the letter *D* if they are DIFFERENT.

CIRCLE
CORRECT ANSWER

1.	111 Caroline Pl Armnk	111 Caroline Pl Armnk	A	D
2.	21 Grnleaf Rye	121 Grnleaf Rye	A	D
3.	245 Rumsy Rd Ynkrs	245 Rumsey Rd Ynkrs	A	D
4.	927 South Peekskl	927 South Pekskl	A	D
5.	44 Monro Av Lrchmt	44 Monroe Av Lrchmt	A	D
6.	39 Andrea Ln Scrsdl	39 Andrea La Scrsdl	A	D
7.	Ruland Wy 62143	Ruland Wy 62143	A	D
8.	51 Cyprs Rd Tukaho	51 Cyprs Rd Tuckaho	A	D
9.	213 Shore Lane Rd Mahopc	213 Shore Lane Av Mahopc	A	D
10.	189 Colmbs Av Lk Oscawna	189 Columbus Av Lk Oscawna	A	D
11.	124 West Stationery Rd	124 West Stationary Rd	A	D
12.	Purdy Vt 03124	Purdy Vt 03124	A	D
13.	129 Tewksbury Rd	129 Twksbury Rd	A	D
14.	Gallow Hill Rd SW	Gallow Hill Rd	A	D
15.	234 Myrtle Av	234 Myrtl Av	A	D
16.	35 Chase Pl NE	35 Chse Pl NE	A	D
17.	14 Terace Av	41 Terace Av	A	D
18.	Collins Pt Rd SE	Colins Pt Rd SE	A	D
19.	164 Sagmor Ct	164 Sagmor Ct	A	D
20.	117 Warburtn Dr NE	117 Wrburtn Dr NE	A	D

KEY (CORRECT ANSWERS)

1. A	6. D	11. D	16. D
2. D	7. A	12. A	17. D
3. D	8. D	13. D	18. D
4. D	9. D	14. D	19. A
5. D	10. D	15. D	20. D

NAME AND NUMBER CHECKING
EXAMINATION SECTION
TEST 1

DIRECTIONS: Each question or incomplete statement is followed by several suggested answers or completions. Select the one that BEST answers the question or completes the statement. *PRINT THE LETTER OF THE CORRECT ANSWER IN THE SPACE AT THE RIGHT.*

Questions 1-10.

DIRECTIONS: Questions 1 through 10 below present the identification numbers, initials, and last names of employees enrolled in a city retirement system. You are to choose the option (A, B, C, or D) that has the identical identification number, initials, and last name as those given in each question.

<u>SAMPLE QUESTION</u>

B145695 JL Jones
- A. B146798 JL Jones
- B. B145698 JL Jonas
- C. P145698 JL Jones
- C. B145698 JL Jones

The correct answer is D. Only option D shows the identification number, initials, and last name exactly as they are in the sample question. Options A, B, and C have errors in the identification number or last name.

1. J297483 PL Robinson
   - A. J294783 PL Robinson
   - B. J297483 PL Robinson
   - C. K297483 PL Robinson
   - D. J297843 PL Robinson

   1.____

2. S497662 JG Schwartz
   - A. S497662 JG Schwarz
   - B. S497762 JG Schwartz
   - C. S497662 JG Schwartz
   - D. S497663 JG Schwartz

   2.____

3. G696436 LN Alberton
   - A. G696436 LM Alberton
   - B. G696436 LN Albertson
   - C. G696346 LN Albertson
   - D. G696436 LN Alberton

   3.____

4. R774923 AD Aldrich
   - A. R774923 AD Aldrich
   - B. R744923 AD Aldrich
   - C. R774932 AP Aldrich
   - D. R774932 AD Allrich

   4.____

5. N239638 RP Hrynyk
   - A. N236938 PR Hrynyk
   - B. N236938 RP Hrynyk
   - C. N239638 PR Hrynyk
   - D. N239638 RP Hrynyk

   5.____

6. R156949 LT Carlson
   A. R156949 LT Carlton
   B. R156494 LT Carlson
   C. R159649 LT Carlton
   D. R156949 LT Carlson

7. T524697 MN Orenstein
   A. T524697 MN Orenstein
   B. T524967 MN Orinstein
   C. T524697 NM Ornstein
   D. T524967 NM Orenstein

8. L346239 JD Remsen
   A. L346239 JD Remson
   B. L364239 JD Remsen
   C. L346438 JD Remsen
   D. L346239 JD Remsen

9. P966438 SB Rieperson
   A. P966438 SB Reiperson
   B. P966438 SB Reiperson
   C. R996438 SB Rieperson
   D. P966438 SB Rieperson

10. D749382 CD Thompson
    A. P749382 CD Thompson
    B. D749832 CD Thomsonn
    C. D749382 CD Thompson
    D. D749823 CD Thomspon

Questions 11-20.

DIRECTIONS: Each of Questions 11 through 20 gives the identification number and name of a person who has received treatment at a certain hospital. You are to choose the option (A, B, C, or D) which has EXACTLY the same identification number and name as those given in the question.

SAMPLE QUESTION

123765 Frank Y. Jones
A. 123675 Frank Y. Jones
B. 123765 Frank T. Jones
C. 123765 Frank Y. Johns
D. 123765 Frank Y. Jones

The correct answer is D. Only option D shows the identification number and name exactly as they are in the sample question. Option A has a mistake in the identification number. Option B has a mistake in the middle initial of the name. Option C has a mistake in the last name.

Now answer Questions 11 through 20 in the same manner.

11. 754898 Diane Malloy
    A. 745898 Diane Malloy
    B. 754898 Dion Malloy
    C. 754898 Diane Malloy
    D. 754898 Diane Maloy

12. 661818 Ferdinand Figueroa
    A. 661818 Ferdinand Figeuroa
    B. 661618 Ferdinand Figueroa
    C. 661818 Ferdnand Figueroa
    D. 661818 Ferdinand Figueroa

3 (#1)

13. 100101 Norman D. Braustein   13.____
    A. 100101 Norman D. Braustein   B. 101001 Norman D. Braustein
    C. 100101 Norman P. Braustien   D. 100101 Norman D. Bruastein

14. 838696 Robert Kittredge   14.____
    A. 838969 Robert Kittredge   B. 838696 Robert Kittredge
    C. 388696 Robert Kittredge   D. 838696 Robert Kittridge

15. 243716 Abraham Soletsky   15.____
    A. 243716 Abrahm Soletsky   B. 243716 Abraham Solestky
    C. 243176 Abraham Soletsky   D. 243716 Abraham Soletsky

16. 981121 Phillip M. Maas   16.____
    A. 981121 Phillip M. Mass   B. 981211 Phillip M. Maas
    C. 981121 Phillip M. Maas   D. 981121 Phillip N. Maas

17. 786556 George Macalusso   17.____
    A. 785656 George Macalusso   B. 786556 George Macalusso
    C. 786556 George Maculasso   D. 786556 George Macluasso

18. 639472 Eugene Weber   18.____
    A. 639472 Eugene Weber   B. 639472 Eugene Webre
    C. 693472 Eugene Weber   D. 639742 Eugene Weber

19. 724936 John J. Lomonaco   19.____
    A. 724936 John J. Lomanoco   B. 724396 John J. Lomonaco
    C. 724936 John J. Lomonaco   D. 724936 John J. Lamonaco

20. 899868 Michael Schnitzer   20.____
    A. 899868 Micheal Schnitzer   B. 898968 Michael Schnizter
    C. 899688 Michael Schnitzer   D. 899868 Michael Schnitzer

Questions 21-28.

DIRECTIONS: Questions 21 through 28 consist of lines of names, dates, and numbers which represent the names, membership dates, social security numbers, and members of the retirement system. For each question you are to choose the option (A, B, C, or D) which exactly matches the information in the question.

SAMPLE QUESTION

Crossen 12/23/56 173568929 25349
  A. Crossen 2/23/56 173568929 253492
  B. Crossen 12/23/56 173568719 253492
  C. Crossen 12/23/56 173568929 253492
  D. Crossan 12/23/56 173568929 258492

4 (#1)

The correct answer is C. Only option C shows the name, date, and numbers exactly as they are in Column I. Option A has a mistake in the date. Option B has a mistake in the social security number. Option D has a mistake in the name and in the membership number.

21. Figueroa 1/15/64 119295386   21.____
    A. Figueroa 1/5/64 119295386 147563
    B. Figueroa 1/15/64 119295386 147563
    C. Figueroa 1/15/64 119295836 147563
    D. Figueroa 1/15/64 119295886 147563

22. Goodridge 6/19/59 106237869 128352   22.____
    A. Goodridge 6/19/59 106287869 128332
    B. Goodrigde 6/19/59 106237869 128352
    C. Goodridge 6/9/59 106237869 128352
    D. Goodridge 6/19/59 106237869 128352

23. Balsam 9/13/57 109652382 116938   23.____
    A. Balsan 9/13/57 109652382 116938
    B. Balsam 9/13/57 109652382 116938
    C. Balsom 9/13/57 109652382 116938
    D. Balsalm 9/13/57 109652382 116938

24. Mackenzie 2/16/49 127362513 101917   24.____
    A. Makenzie 2/16/49 127362513 101917
    B. Mackenzie 2/16/49 127362513 101917
    C. Mackenzie 2/16/49 127362513 101977
    D. Mackenzie 2/16/49 127862513 101917

25. Halpern 12/2/73 115205359 286070   25.____
    A. Halpern 12/2/73 115206359 286070
    B. Halpern 12/2/73 113206359 286070
    C. Halpern 12/2/73 115206359 206870
    D. Halpern 12/2/73 115206359 286870

26. Phillips 4/8/66 137125516 192612   26.____
    A. Phillips 4/8/66 137125516 196212
    B. Philipps 4/8/66 137125516 192612
    C. Phillips 4/8/66 137125516 192612
    D. Phillips 4/8/66 137122516 192612

27. Francisce 11/9/63 123926037 152210   27.____
    A. Francisce 11/9/63 123826837 152210
    B. Francisce 11/9/63 123926037 152210
    C. Francisce 11/9/63 123936037 152210
    D. Franscice 11/9/63 123926037 152210

28. Silbert 7/28/54 118421999 178514
   A. Silbert 7/28/54 118421999 178544
   B. Silbert 7/28/54 184421999 178514
   C. Silbert 7/28/54 118421999 178514
   D. Siblert 7/28/54 118421999 178514

28.____

KEY (CORRECT ANSWERS)

1.	B	11.	C	21.	B
2.	C	12.	D	22.	D
3.	D	13.	A	23.	B
4.	A	14.	B	24.	B
5.	D	15.	D	25.	A
6.	D	16.	C	26.	C
7.	A	17.	B	27.	B
8.	D	18.	A	28.	C
9.	D	19.	C		
10.	C	20.	D		

TEST 2

DIRECTIONS: Each question or incomplete statement is followed by several suggested answers or completions. Select the one that BEST answers the question or completes the statement. *PRINT THE LETTER OF THE CORRECT ANSWER IN THE SPACE AT THE RIGHT.*

Questions 1-3.

DIRECTIONS: Items 1 through 3 are a test of your proofreading ability. Each item consists of Copy I and Copy II. You are to assume that Copy I in each item is correct. Copy II, which is meant to be a duplicate of Copy I, may contain some typographical errors. In each item, compare Copy II with Copy I and determine the number of errors in Copy II. If there are:
no errors, mark your answer A;
1 or 2 errors, mark your answer B;
3 or 4 errors, mark your answer C;
5 or 6 errors, mark your answer D;
7 errors or more, mark your answer E.

1.
COPY I
The Commissioner, before issuing any such license, shall cause an investigation to be made of the premises named and described in such application, to determine whether all the provisions of the sanitary code, building code, state industrial code, state minimum wage law, local laws, regulations of municipal agencies, and other requirements of this article are fully observed. (Section B32-169.0 of Article 23.)

COPY II
The Commissioner, before issuing any such license shall cause an investigation to be made of the premises named and described in such application, to determine whether all the provisions of the sanitary code, bilding code, state industrial code, state minimum wage laws, local laws, regulations of municipal agencies, and other requirements of this article are fully observed. (Section E32-169.0 of Article 23.)

1.____

2.
COPY I
Among the persons who have been appointed to various agencies are John Queen, 9 West 55th Street, Brooklyn; Joseph Blount, 2497 Durward Road, Bronx; Lawrence K. Eberhardt, 3194 Bedford Street, Manhattan; Reginald L. Darcy, 1476 Allerton Drive, Bronx; and Benjamin Ledwith, 177 Greene Street, Manhattan.

2.____

COPY II
Among the persons who have been appointed to various agencies are John Queen, 9 West 56th Street, Brooklyn, Joseph Blount, 2497 Dureward Road, Bronx: Lawrence K. Eberhart, 3194 Belford Street, Manhattan; Reginald L. Barcey, 1476 Allerton drive, Bronx; and Benjamin Ledwith, 177 Green Street, Manhattan.

3.
COPY I
Except as hereinafter provided, it shall be unlawful to use, store or have on hand any inflammable motion picture film in quantities greater than one standard or two sub-standard reels, or aggregating more than two thousand feet in length, or more than ten pounds in weight without the permit required by this section.

COPY II
Except as herinafter provided, it shall be unlawful to use, store or have on hand any inflamable motion picture film, in quantities greater than one standard or two substandard reels or aggregating more than two thousand feet in length, or more than ten pounds in weight without the permit required by this section.

3.____

Questions 4-6.

DIRECTIONS: Items 4 through 6 are a test of your proofreading ability. Each question consists of Copy I and Copy II. You are to assume that Copy I in each question is correct. Copy II, which is meant to be a duplicate of Copy I, may contain some typographical errors. In each question, compare Copy II with Copy I and determine the number of errors in Copy II. If there are:
no errors, mark your answer A;
1 or 2 errors, mark your answer B;
3 or 4 errors, mark your answer C;
5 or 6 errors or more, mark your answer D;

4.
COPY I
It shall be unlawful to install wires or appliances for electric light, heat or power, operating at a potential in excess of seven hundred fifty volts, in or on any part of a building, with the exception of a central station, sub-station, transformer, or switching vault, or motor room; provided, however, that the Commissioner may authorize the use of radio transmitting apparatus under special conditions.

COPY II
It shall be unlawful to install wires or appliances for electric light, heat or power, operating at a potential in excess of seven hundred fifty volts, in or on any part of a building, with the exception of a central station, sub-station, transformer, or switching vault, or motor room, provided, however, that the Commissioner may authorize the use of radio transmitting apperatus under special conditions.

4.____

3 (#2)

5.

COPY I
The grand total debt service for the fiscal year 2006-27 amounts to $350,563,718.63, as compared with $309,561,347.27 for the current fiscal year, or an increase of $41,002,371.36. The amount payable from other sources in 2006-07 shows an increase of $13,264,165.47, resulting in an increase of $27,733,205.89 payable from tax levy funds.

COPY II
The grand total debt service for the fiscal year 2006-07 amounts to $350,568,718.63, as compared with $309,561,347.27 for the current fiscel year, or an increase of $41,002,371.36. The amount payable from other sources in 2006-07 show an increase of $13,264,165.47 resulting in an increase of $27,733,295.89 payable from tax levy funds.

5.____

6.

COPY I
The following site proposed for the new building is approximately rectangular in shape and comprises an entire block, having frontages of about 721 feet on 16th Road, 200 feet on 157th feet, 721 on 17th Avenue and 200 feet on 154th Street, with a gross area of about 144,350 square feet. The 2006-07 assessed valuation is $28,700,000 of which $6,000,000 is for improvements.

COPY II
The following site proposed for the new building is approximately rectangular in shape and comprises an entire block, having frontage of about 721 feet on 16th Road, 200 feet on 157th Street on 17th Avenue, and 200 feet on 134th Street, with a gross area of about 114,350 square feet. The 2006-07 assessed valuation is $28,700,000 of which $6,000,000 is for improvements.

6.____

KEY (CORRECT ANSWERS)

1. D   4. B
2. E   5. D
3. E   6. C

TEST 3

DIRECTIONS: Each question or incomplete statement is followed by several suggested answers or completions. Select the one that BEST answers the question or completes the statement. *PRINT THE LETTER OF THE CORRECT ANSWER IN THE SPACE AT THE RIGHT.*

Questions 1-8.

DIRECTIONS: Each of the questions numbered 1 through 8 consists of three sets of names and name codes. In each question, the two names and name codes on the same line are supposed to be exactly the same.
Look carefully at each set of names and cods and mark your answer
A. if there are mistakes in all three sets
B. if there are mistakes in two of the sets
C. if there is a mistake in only one set
D. if there are no mistakes in any of the sets

SAMPLE QUESTION

The following sample question is given to help you understand the procedure.

Macabe, John N. – V53162	Macade, John N. – V53162
Howard, Joan S. – J24791	Howard, Joan S. – J24791
Ware, Susan B. – A45068	Ware, Susan B. – A45968

In the above sample question, the names and name codes of the first set are not exactly the same because of the spelling of the last name (Macabe – Macade). The names and name codes of the second set are exactly the same. The names and name codes of the third set are not exactly the same because the two name codes are different (A45068 – A45968). Since there are mistakes in only 2 of the sets, the answer to the sample question is B.

1. Powell, Michael C. – 78537F   Powell, Michael C. – 78537F   1.____
    Martinez, Pablo J. – 24435P   Martinez, Pablo J. – 24435P
    MacBane, Eliot M. – 98674E   MacBane, Eliot M. – 98674E

2. Fitz-Kramer Machines, Inc. – 259090   Fitz-Kramer Machines, Inc. – 259090   2.____
    Marvel Cleaning Service – 482657   Marvel Cleaning Service – 482657
    Donato, Carl G. – 637418   Danato, Carl G. - 687418

3. Martin Davison Trading Corp – 43108T   Martin Davidson Trading Corp. – 43108T   3.____
    Cotwald Lighting Fixtures -76065L   Cotwald Lighting Fixtures – 70056L
    R. Crawford Plumbers – 23157C   R. Crawford Plumbers – 23157G

4. Fraiman Engineering Corp. – M4773   Friaman Engineering Corp. – M4773   4.____
    Neuman, Walter B. – N7745   Neumen, Walter B. – N7745
    Pierce, Eric M. – W6304   Pierce, Eric M. – W6304

5. Constable, Eugene – B64837   Comstable, Eugene – B6437   5.____
    Derrick, Paul – H27119   Derrik, Paul – H27119
    Heller, Karen – S4966   Heller, Karen – S46906

6. Hernando Delivery Service Co. - D7456   Hernando Delivery Service Co. – D7456   6.____
    Barettz Electrical Supplies - N5392   Barettz Electrical Supplies – N5392
    Tanner, Abraham – M4798   Tanner, Abraham – M4798

7. Kalin Associates – R38641   Kaline Associates – R38641   7.____
    Sealey, Robert E. – P63533   Sealey, Robert E. – P63553
    Seals! Office Furniture – R36742   Seals! Office Furniture – R36742

8. Janowsky, Philip M. – 742213   Janowsky, Philip M. – 742213   8.____
    Hansen, Thomas H. – 934816   Hanson, Thomas H. – 934816
    L. Lester and Son Inc. – 294568   L. Lester and Son Inc. - 294568

Questions 9-13.

DIRECTIONS: Each of the questions numbered 9 through 13 consists of three sets of names and building codes. In each question, the two names and building codes on the same line are supposed to be exactly the same.
If you find an error or errors on only one of the sets in the question, mark your answer A; any two of the sets in the question, mark your answer B; all three of the sets in the question, mark your answer C; none of the sets, mark your answer D.

SAMPLE QUESTION

Column I
Duvivier, Anne P. – X52714
Dyrborg, Alfred – B4217
Dymnick, JoAnne – P482596

Column II
Duviver, Anne P. – X52714
Dyrborg, Alfred – B4267
Dymnick, JoAnne – P482596

In the above sample question, the first set of names and building codes is not exactly the same because the last names are spelled differently (Duvivier – Duviver). The second set of names and building codes is not exactly the same because the building codes are different (B4217 – B4267). The third set of names and building codes is exactly the same. Since there are mistakes in two of the sets of names and building codes, the answer to the sample question is B.

Now answer the questions using the same procedure.

Column I
9. Lautmann, Gerald G. – C2483
    Lawlor, Michael – W44639
    Lawrence, John J. – H1358

Column II
    Lautmann, Gerald C. – C2483   9.____
    Lawler, Michael – W44639
    Lawrence, John J. – H1358

3 (#3)

Column I	Column II	
10. Mittmann, Howard – J4113 Mitchell, William T. – M75271 Milan, T. Thomas – Q67553	Mittmann, Howard – J4113 Mitchell, William T. – M75721 Milan, T. Thomas – Q67553	10.____
11. Quarles, Vincent – J34760 Quinn, Alan N. – S38813 Quinones, Peter W. – B87467	Quarles, Vincent – J34760 Quinn, Alan N. – S38813 Quinones, Peter W. – B87467	11.____
12. Daniels, Harold H. – A26554 Dantzler, Richard – C35780 Davidson, Martina – E62901	Daniels, Harold H – A26544 Dantzler, Richard – 035780 Davidson, Martin – E62901	12.____
13. Graham, Cecil J. – I20244 Granger, Deborah – T86211 Grant, Charles L. – G5788	Graham, Cecil J. – I20244 Granger, Deborah – T86211 Grant, Charles L. – G5788	13.____

KEY (CORRECT ANSWERS)

1.	D	6.	D	11.	D
2.	C	7.	B	12.	C
3.	A	8.	C	13.	D
4.	B	9.	B		
5.	A	10.	A		

TEST 4

DIRECTIONS: In Questions 1 through 10 there are five pairs of numbers or letters and numbers. Compare each pair and decide how many pairs are exactly alike. *PRINT THE LETTER OF THE CORRECT ANSWER IN THE SPACE AT THE RIGHT.*

    A. if only one pair is exactly alike
    B. if only two pairs are exactly alike
    C. if only three pairs are exactly alike
    D. if only four pairs are exactly alike
    E. if all five pairs are exactly alike.

1. 73-F.....F-73   FF-73.....FF-73   1.____
   F-7373.....F-7373   373-FF.....337-FF
   F-733.....337-F

2. 0-17158.....0-17158   0-71518.....0-71518   2.____
   0-11758.....0-11758   0-15817.....0-15817

3. 1A-7908.....1A-7908   7A-8901.....7A-8091   3.____
   71-891.....7A-891   1A-9078.....1A-9708
   9A-7018.....9A-7081

4. 2V-6426.....2V-6246   2N-6246.....2N-6246   4.____
   2V-6426.....2N-6426   2N-6624.....2N-6624
   2V-6462.....2V-6562

5. 3NY-56.....3NY-65   5NY-356.....3NY-356   5.____
   6NY-3566.....3NY-3566   5NY-6536.....5NY-6536
   3NY-5663.....5NY-3663

6. COB-065.....COB-065   BCL-506.....BCL-506   6.____
   LBC-650.....LBC-650   DLB-560.....DLB-560
   CDB-056.....COB-065

7. 4KQ-9130.....4KQ-9130   4KQ-9310.....4KQ-9130   7.____
   4KQ-9031.....4KQ-9301   4KQ-9301.....4KQ-9301
   4KQ-9013.....4KQ-9013

8. MK-89.....MK-98   98-MK.....89-MK   8.____
   MSK-998.....MSK-998   MOSK.....MOKS
   SMK-899.....SMK-899

9. 8MD-2104.....SMD-2014   2MD-8140.....2MD-8140   9.____
   814-MD.....814-MD   4MD-8201.....4MD-8201
   MD-281.....MD-481

10. 161-035.....161-035   150-316.....150-316   10.____
    315-160.....315-160   131-650.....131-650
    165-301.....165-301

KEY (CORRECT ANSWERS)

1. B
2. E
3. B
4. C
5. A
6. D
7. D
8. B
9. C
10. E

TEST 5

DIRECTIONS: Each question or incomplete statement is followed by several suggested answers or completions. Select the one that BEST answers the question or completes the statement. *PRINT THE LETTER OF THE CORRECT ANSWER IN THE SPACE AT THE RIGHT.*

Questions -5.

DIRECTIONS: Questions 1 through 5, inclusive, consist of groups of four displays representing license identification plates. Examine each group of plates and determine the number of plates in each group which are identical. Mark your answer sheets as follows:
    If only two plates are identical, mark answer A.
    If only three plates are identical, mark answer B.
    If all four plates are identical, mark answer C.
    If the plates are all different, mark answer D.

EXAMPLE
ABC123   BCD123   ABC123   BCD235

Since only two plates are identical, the first and third, the correct answer is A.

1. PBV839   PVB839   PVB839   PVB839   1.____

2. WTX083   WTX083   WTX083   WTX083   2.____

3. B73609   D73906   BD7396   BD7906   3.____

4. AK7423   AK7423   AK1423   A81324   4.____

5. 583Y10   683Y10   583701   583710   5.____

Questions 6-10.

DIRECTIONS: Questions 6 through 10 consist of groups of numbers and letters similar to those which might appear on license plates. Each group of numbers and letters will be called a license identification. Choose the license identification lettered A, B, C, or D that EXACTLY matches the license identification shown next to the question number.

SAMPLE
NY 1977
ABC-123

A. NY 1976   B. NY 1977   C. NY 1977   D. NY 1977
    ABC-123   ABC-132   CBA-123   ABC-123

2 (#5)

The license identification given is NY 1977.
ABC-123
The only choice that exactly matches it is the license identification next to the letter D. The correct answer is therefore D.

6.   NY 1976
                              QLT-781   6.____

    A. NJ 1976   B. NY 1975   C. NY 1976   D. NY 1977
       QLT-781   QLT-781   QLT-781   QLT-781

7.   FLA 1977
                            2-7LT58J   7.____

    A. FLA 1977   B. FLA 1977   C. FLA 1977   D. LA 1977
       2-7TL58J   2-7LTJ58   2-7LT58J   2-7LT58J

8.   NY 1975
                            OQC383   8.____

    A. NY 1975   B. NY 1975   C. NY 1975   D. NY 1977
       OQC383   OQC833   QCQ383   OCQ383

9.   MASS 1977
                            B-8DK02   9.____

    A. MISS 1977   B. MASS 1977   C. MASS 1976   D. MASS 1977
       B-8DK02   B-8DK02   B-8DK02   B-80KD2

10.   NY 1976
                         ZV0586   10.____

    A. NY 1976   B. NY 1977   C. NY 1975   D. NY 1976
       2V-0586   ZV0586   ZV0586   ZU0586

KEY (CORRECT ANSWERS)

1. B   6. C
2. C   7. C
3. D   8. A
4. A   9. B
5. A   10. C

TEST 6

DIRECTIONS: Assume that each of the capital letters in the table below represent the name of an employee enrolled in the city employees' retirement system. The number directly beneath the letter represents the agency for which the employee works, and the small letter directly beneath represents the code for the employee's account.

Name of Employee	L	O	T	Q	A	M	R	N	C
Agency	3	4	5	9	8	7	2	1	6
Account Code	r	f	b	i	d	t	g	e	n

In each of the following questions 1 through 3, the agency code numbers and the account code letters in Columns 2 and 3 should correspond to the capital letters in Column 1 and should be in the same consecutive order. For each question, look at each column carefully and mark your answer as follows:
If there are one or more errors in Column 2 only, mark your answer A.
If there are one or more errors in Column 3 only, mark your answer B.
If there are one or more errors in Column 2 and one or more errors in Column 3, mark your answer C.
If there are NO errors in either column, mark your answer D.
The following sample question is given to help you understand the procedure.

Column 1	Column 2	Column 3
TQLMOC	583746	birtfn

In Column 2, the second agency code number (corresponding to letter Q) should be "9", not "8". Column 3 is coded correctly to Column 1. Since there is an error only in Column 2, the correct answer is A.

	Column 1	Column 2	Column 3	
1.	QLNRCA	931268	iregnd	1.____
2.	NRMOTC	127546	egftbn	2.____
3.	RCTALM	265837	gndbrt	3.____

KEY (CORRECT ANSWERS)

1. D
2. C
3. B

NAME AND NUMBER CHECKING
EXAMINATION SECTION
TEST 1

DIRECTIONS: This test is designed to measure your speed/and accuracy. You are urged to work both quickly and accurately and to do correctly as many lists as you can in the time allowed. The test consists of lists or pairs of names and numbers. Count the number of IDENTICAL pairs in each list. Then, select the correct number, 1, 2, 3, 4, 5, and indicate your choice in the space at the right. Two sample questions are presented for your guidance, together with the correct solutions.

SAMPLE LIST A
Adelphi College   – Adelphia College
Braxton Corp   – Braxeton Corp.
Wassaic State School   – Wassaic State School
Central Islip State Hospital   – Central Isllip State Hospital
Greenwich House   – Greenwich House

NOTE: There are only two correct pairs—Wassaic State School and Greenwich House. Therefore, the CORRECT answer is 2.

SAMPLE LIST B
78453694   – 78453684
784530   – 784530
533   – 534
67845   – 67845
2368745   – 2368755

NOTE: There are only two correct pairs—784530 and 67845. Therefore, the CORRECT answer is 2.

LIST 1   1.____
    98654327   - 98654327
    74932564   - 7492564
    61438652   - 61438652
    01297653   - 01287653
    1865439765   - 1865439765

LIST 2   2.____
    478362   - 478363
    278354792   - 278354772
    9327   - 9327
    297384625   - 27384625
    6428156   - 6428158

2 (#1)

LIST 3 3.____
    Abbey House   - Abbey House
    Actor's Fund Home   - Actor's Fund Home
    Adrian Memorial   - Adrian Memorial
    A. Clayton Powell Home   - Clayton Powell House
    Abbot E. Kittredge Club - Abbott E. Kitteredge Club

LIST 4 4.____
    3682   - 3692
    21937453829   - 31927453829
    723   - 733
    2763920   - 2763920
    47293   - 47293

LIST 5 5.____
    Adra House   - Adra House
    Adolescents' Court   - Adolescents' Court
    Cliff Villa   - Cliff Villa
    Clark Neighborhood House - Clark Neighborhood House
    Alma Mathews House   - Alma Mathews House

LIST 6 6.____
    28734291   - 28734271
    63810263849   - 63810263846
    26831027   - 26831027
    368291   - 368291
    7238102637   - 7238102637

LIST 7 7.____
    Albion State T.S.   - Albion State T.C.
    Clara de Hirsch Home   - Clara De Hirsch Home
    Alice Carrington Royce - Alice Carington Royce
    Alice Chopin Nursery   - Alice Chapin Nursery
    Lighthouse Eye Clinic   - Lighthouse Eye Clinic

LIST 8 8.____
    327   - 329
    712438291026   - 712438291026
    2753829142   - 275382942
    826287   - 826289
    26435162839   - 26435162839

LIST 9 9.____
    Letchworth Village   - Letchworth Village
    A.A.A.E. Inc.   - A.A.A.E. Inc.
    Clear Pool Camp   - Clear Pool Camp
    A.M.M.L.A. Inc.   - A.M.M.L.A. Inc.
    J.G. Harbard   - J.G. Harbord

3 (#1)

LIST 10   10.____
   8254   - 8256
   2641526   - 2641526
   4126389012   - 4126389102
   725   - 725
   76253917287   - 76253917287

LIST 11   11.____
   Attica State Prison   - Attica State Prison
   Nellie Murrah   - Nellie Murrah
   Club Marshall   - Club Marshal
   Assissium Casea-Maria - Assissium Casa-Maria
   The Homestead   - The Homestead

LIST 12   12.____
   2691   - 2691
   623819253627 - 623819253629
   28637   - 28937
   278392736   - 278392736
   52739   - 52739

LIST 13   13.____
   A.I.C.P. Boys Camp   - A.I.C.P. Boy's Camp
   Einar Chrystie   - Einar Christyie
   Astoria Center   - Astoria Center
   G. Frederick Brown   - G. Federick Browne
   Vacation Service   - Vacation Services

LIST 14   14.____
   728352689   - 728352688
   643728   - 643728
   37829176   - 37827196
   8425367   - 8425369
   65382018   - 65382018

LIST 15   15.____
   E.S. Streim   - E.S. Strim
   Charles E. Higgins - Charles E. Higgins
   Baluvelt, N.Y.   - Blauwelt, N.Y.
   Roberta Magdalen   - Roberto Magdalen
   Ballard School   - Ballard School

LIST 16   16.____
   7382   - 7392
   281374538299 - 291374538299
   623   - 633
   6273730   - 6273730
   63392   - 63392

4 (#1)

LIST 17   17.____
    Orrin Otis — - Orrin Otis
    Barat Settlement — - Barat Settlemen
    Emmanuel House — - Emmanuel House
    William T. McCreery — - William T. McCreery
    Seamen's Home — - Seaman's Home

LIST 18   18.____
    72824391 — - 72834371
    3729106237 — - 37291106237
    82620163849 — - 82620163846
    37638921 — - 37638921
    82631027 — - 82631027

LIST 19   19.____
    Commonwealth Fund — - Commonwealth Fund
    Anne Johnsen — - Anne Johnson
    Bide-A-Wee Home — - Bide-a-Wee Home
    Riverdale-on-Hudson — - Riverdal-on-Hudson
    Bialystoker Home — - Bailystoker Home

LIST 20   20.____
    9271 — - 9271
    392918352627 — - 392018852629
    72637 — - 72637
    927392736 — - 927392736
    92739 — - 92739

LIST 21   21.____
    Charles M. Stump — - Charles M. Stump
    Bourne Workshop — - Buorne Workshop
    B'nai Bi'rith — - B'nai Brith
    Poppenhuesen Institute — - Poppenheusen Institute
    Consular Service — - Consular Service

LIST 22   22.____
    927352689 — - 927352688
    647382 — - 648382
    93729176 — - 93727196
    649536718 — - 649536718
    5835367 — - 5835369

LIST 23   23.____
    L.S. Bestend — - L.S. Bestent
    Hirsch Mfg. Co. — - Hircsh Mfg. Co.
    F.H. Storrs — - F.P. Storrs
    Camp Wassaic — - Camp Wassaic
    George Ballingham — - George Ballingham

5 (#1)

LIST 24
   372846392048   - 372846392048
   334   - 334
   7283524678   - 7283524678
   7283   - 7283
   7283629372   - 7283629372

24.____

LIST 25
   Dr. Stiles Company   - Dr. Stills Company
   Frances Hunsdon   - Frances Hunsdon
   Northrop Barrert   - Nothrup Barrent
   J.D. Brunjes   - J.D. Brunjes
   Theo. Claudel & Co.   - Theo. Claudel co.

25.____

KEY (CORRECT ANSWERS)

1.	3	11.	3
2.	1	12.	3
3.	2	13.	1
4.	2	14.	2
5.	5	15.	2
6.	3	16.	2
7.	1	17.	3
8.	2	18.	2
9.	4	19.	2
10.	3	20.	4

21.	2
22.	1
23.	2
24.	5
25.	2

TEST 2

DIRECTIONS: This test is designed to measure your speed/and accuracy. You are urged to work both quickly and accurately and to do correctly as many lists as you can in the time allowed. The test consists of lists or pairs of names and numbers. Count the number of IDENTICAL pairs in each list. Then, select the correct number, 1, 2, 3, 4, 5, and indicate your choice in the space at the right.

LIST 1
    82728   - 82738
    82736292637   - 82736292639
    728   - 738
    83926192527   - 83726192529
    82736272   - 82736272

1.____

LIST 2
    L. Pietri   - L. Pietri
    Mathewson, L.F.   - Mathewson, L.F.
    Funk & Wagnall   - Funk & Wagnalls
    Shimizu, Sojio   - Shimizu, Sojio
    Filing Equipment Bureau - Filing Equipment Buraeu

2.____

LIST 3
    63801829374   - 63801839474
    283577657   - 283577657
    65689   - 65689
    3457892026   - 3547893026
    2779   - 2778

3.____

LIST 4
    August Caille   - August Caille
    The Well-Fare Service   - The Wel-Fare Service
    K.L.M. Process co.   - R.L.M. Process Co.
    Merrill Littell   - Merrill Littell
    Dodd & Sons   - Dodd & Son

4.____

LIST 5
    998745732   - 998745733
    723   - 723
    463849102983   - 463849102983
    8570   - 8570
    279012   - 279012

5.____

LIST 6
    M.A. Wender   - M.A. Winder
    Minneapolis Supply Co. - Minneapolis Supply Co.
    Beverly Hills Corp   - Beverley Hills Corp.
    Trafalgar Square   - Trafalgar Square
    Phifer, D.T.   - Phiefer, D.T.

6.____

2 (#2)

LIST 7   7._____
   7834629   - 7834629
   3549806746   - 3549806746
   97802564   - 97892564
   689246   - 688246
   2578024683   - 2578024683

LIST 8   8._____
   Scadrons'   - Scadrons'
   Gensen & Bro.   - Genson & Bro.
   Firestone Co.   - Firestone Co.
   H.L. Eklund   - H.L. Eklund
   Oleomargarine Co.   - Oleomargarine Co.

LIST 9   9._____
   782039485618   - 782039485618
   53829172639   - 63829172639
   892   - 892
   82937482   - 829374820
   52937456   - 53937456

LIST 10   10._____
   First Nat'l Bank   - First Nat'l Bank
   Sedgwick Machine Works   - Sedgewick Machine Works
   Hectographia Co.   - Hectographia Corp.
   Levet Bros.   - Levet Bros.
   Multistamp Co., Inc.   - Multistamp Co., Inc.

LIST 11   11._____
   7293   - 7293
   6382910293   - 6382910292
   981928374012   - 981928374912
   58293   - 58393
   18203649271   - 283019283745

LIST 12   12._____
   Lowrey Lb'r Co.   - Lowrey Lb'r Co.
   Fidelity Service   - Fidelity Service
   Reumann, J.A.   - Reumann, J.A.
   Duophoto Ltd.   - Duophotos Ltd.
   John Jarratt   - John Jaratt

LIST 13   13._____
   6820384   - 6820384
   383019283745   - 383019283745
   63927102   - 63928102
   91029354829   - 91029354829
   58291728   - 58291728

LIST 14   14._____
    Standard Press Co.   - Standard Press Co.
    Reliant Mf'g. Co.   - Relant Mf'g Co.
    M.C. Lynn   - M.C. Lynn
    J. Fredericks Company   - G. Fredericks Company
    Wandermann, B.S.   - Wanderman, B.S.

LIST 15   15._____
    4283910293   - 4283010203
    992018273648   - 992018273848
    620   - 629
    752937273   - 752937373
    5392   - 5392

LIST 16   16._____
    Waldorf Hotel   - Waldorf Hotel
    Aaron Machinery Co.   - Aaron Machinery Co.
    Caroline Ann Locke   - Caroline Ane Locke
    McCabe Mfg. Co.   - McCabe Mfg. Co.
    R.L. Landres   - R.L. Landers

LIST 17   17._____
    68391028364   - 68391028394
    68293   - 68293
    739201   - 739201
    72839201   - 72839211
    739917   - 739719

LIST 18   18._____
    Balsam M.M.   - Balsamm, M.M.
    Steinway & Co.   - Stienway & M. Co.
    Eugene Elliott   - Eugene A. Elliott
    Leonard Loan Co.   - Leonard Loan Co.
    Frederick Morgan   - Frederick Morgen

LIST 19   19._____
    8929   - 9820
    392836472829   - 392836572829
    462   - 4622039271
    827   - 2039276837
    53829   - 54829

LIST 20   20._____
    Danielson's Hofbrau   - Danielson's Hafbrau
    Edward A. Truarme   - Edward A. Truame
    Insulite Co.   - Insulite Co.
    Reisler Shoe Corp.   - Rielser Shoe Corp.
    L.L. Thompson   - L.L. Thompson

4 (#2)

LIST 21   21.____
    92839102837   - 92839102837
    58891028   - 58891028
    7291728   - 7291928
    272839102839   - 272839102839
    428192   - 428102

LIST 22   22.____
    K.L. Veiller   - K.L. Veiller
    Webster, Roy   - Webster, Ray
    Drasner Spring Co.   - Drasner Spring Co.
    Edward J. Cravenport   - Edward J. Cravanport
    Harold Field   - Harold A. Field

LIST 23   23.____
    2293   - 2293
    4283910293   - 5382910292
    871928374012   - 871928374912
    68293   - 68393
    8120364927   - 81293649271

LIST 24   24.____
    Tappe, Inc   - Tappe, Inc.
    A.M. Wentingworth   - A.M. Wentinworth
    Scott A. Elliott   - Scott A. Elliott
    Echeverria Corp.   - Echeverria Corp.
    Bradford Victor Company   - Bradford Victer Company

LIST 25   25.____
    4820384   - 4820384
    393019283745   - 283919283745
    63917102   - 63927102
    91029354829   - 91029354829
    48291728   - 48291728

KEY (CORRECT ANSWERS)

1.	1	11.	1
2.	3	12.	3
3.	2	13.	4
4.	2	14.	2
5.	4	15.	1
6.	2	16.	3
7.	3	17.	2
8.	4	18.	1
9.	2	19.	1
10.	3	20.	2

21.	3
22.	2
23.	1
24.	2
25.	4

NAME AND NUMBER CHECKING
EXAMINATION SECTION
TEST 1

DIRECTIONS: Questions 1 through 17 consist of sets of names and addresses. In each question, the name and address in Column II should be an exact copy of the name and address in Column I.
If there is:
a mistake only in the name, mark your answer A;
a mistake only in the address, mark your answer B;
a mistake in both name and address, mark your answer C;
No mistake in either name or address, mark your answer D.

Sample Question

Column I
Christina Magnusson
288 Greene Street
New York, N.Y. 10003

Column II
Christina Magnusson
288 Greene Street
New York, N.Y. 10013

Since there is a mistake only in the address (the zip code should be 10003 instead of 10013), the answer to the sample question is B.

COLUMN I

1. Ms. Joan Kelly
   313 Franklin Avenue
   Brooklyn, N.Y. 11202

2. Mrs. Eileen Engel
   47-24 86 Road
   Queens, N.Y. 11122

3. Marcia Michaels
   213 E. 81 St.
   New York, N.Y. 10012

4. Rev. Edward J. Smyth
   1401 Brandeis Street
   San Francisco, Calif. 96201

5. Alicia Rodriguez
   24-68 82 St.
   Elmhurst, N.Y. 11122

COLUMN II

Ms. Joan Kielly
318 Franklin Ave.
Brooklyn, N.Y. 11202

Mrs. Ellen Engel
47-24 86 Road
Queens, New York 11122

Marcia Michaels
213 E. 81 St.
New York, N.Y. 10012

Rev. Edward J. Smyth
1401 Brandies Street
San Francisco, Calif. 96201

Alicia Rodriguez
2468 81 St.
Elmhurst, N.Y. 11122

1.____

2.____

3.____

4.____

5.____

2 (#1)

COLUMN I	COLUMN II	
6. Ernest Eisemann 21 Columbia St. New York, N.Y. 10007	Ernest Eisermann 21 Columbia St. New York, N.Y. 10007	6.____
7. Mr. & Mrs. George Petersson 87-11 91st Avenue Woodhaven, N.Y. 11421	Mr. & Mrs. George Peterson 87-11 91st Avenue Woodhaven, N.Y. 11421	7.____
8. Mr. Ivan Klebnikov 1848 Newkirk Avenue Brooklyn, N.Y. 11226	Mr. Ivan Klebikov 1848 Newkirk Avenue Brooklyn, N.Y. 11622	8.____
9. Mr. Samuel Rothfleisch 71 Pine Street New York, N.Y. 10005	Samuel Rothfleisch 71 Pine Street New York, N.Y. 100005	9.____
10. Mrs. Isabel Tonnessen 198 East 185th Street Bronx, N.Y. 10458	Mrs. Isabel Tonnessen 189 East 185th Street Bronx, N.Y. 10348	10.____
11. Esteban Perez 173 Eighth Street Staten Island, N.Y. 10306	Estaban Perez 173 Eighth Street Staten Island, N.Y. 10306	11.____
12. Esta Wong 141 West 68 St. New York, N.Y. 10023	Esta Wang 141 West 68 St. New York, N.Y. 10023	12.____
13. Dr. Alberto Grosso 3475 12th Avenue Brooklyn, N.Y. 11218	Dr. Alberto Grosso 3475 12th Avenue Brooklyn, N.Y. 11218	13.____
14. Mrs. Ruth Bortias 482 Theresa Ct. Far Rockaway, N.Y. 11691	Ms. Ruth Bortlas 482 Theresa Ct. Far Rockaway, N.Y. 11169	14.____
15. Mr. & Mrs. Howard Fox 2301 Sedgwick Ave. Bronx, N.Y. 10468	Mr. & Mrs. Howard Fox 231 Sedgwick Ave. Bronx, N.Y. 10468	15.____
16. Miss Marjorie Black 223 East 23 Street New York, N.Y. 10010	Miss Margorie Black 223 East 23 Street New York, N.Y. 10010	16.____

COLUMN I	COLUMN II	
17. Michelle Herman 806 Valley Rd. Old Tappan, N.J. 07675	Michelle Hermann 806 Valley Dr. Old Tappan, N.J. 07675	17.____

KEY (CORRECT ANSWERS)

1.	C	7.	A	13.	D
2.	A	8.	C	14.	C
3.	D	9.	D	15.	B
4.	B	10.	B	16.	A
5.	B	11.	A	17.	C
6.	A	12.	D		

TEST 2

DIRECTIONS: Questions 1 through 15 are to be answered SOLELY on the instructions given below. *PRINT THE LETTER OF THE CORRECT ANSWER IN THE SPACE AT THE RIGHT.*

INSTRUCTIONS

In each of the following questions, the 3-line name and address in Column I is the master-list entry, and the 3-line entry in Column II is the information to be checked against the master list. If there is one line that does not match, mark your answer A; if there are two lines that do not match, mark your answer B; if all three lines do not match, mark your answer C; if the lines all match exactly, mark your answer D.

Sample Question

Column I
Mark L. Field
11-09 Price Park Blvd.
Bronx, N.Y. 11402

Column II
Mark L. Field
11-99 Prince Park Way
Bronx, N.Y. 11401

The first lines in each column match exactly. The second lines do not match since 11-09 does not match 11-<u>99</u>; and Blvd. does not match <u>Way</u>. The third lines do not match either since 1140<u>2</u> does not match 1140<u>1</u>. Therefore, there are two lines that do not match, and the CORRECT answer is B.

COLUMN I

1. Jerome A. Jackson
   1243 14th Avenue
   New York, N.Y. 10023

2. Sophie Strachtheim
   33-28 Connecticut Ave.
   Far Rockaway, N.Y. 11697

3. Elisabeth N.T. Gorrell
   256 Exchange St.
   New York, N.Y. 10013

4. Maria J. Gonzalez
   7516 E. Sheepshead Rd.
   Brooklyn, N.Y. 11240

5. Leslie B. Brautenweiler
   21 57A Seiler Terr.
   Flushing, N.Y. 11367

COLUMN II

Jerome A. Johnson
1234 14th Avenue
New York, N.Y. 10023

Sophie Strachtheim
33-28 Connecticut Ave.
Far Rockaway, N.Y. 11697

Elizabeth N.T. Gorrell
256 Exchange St.
New York, N.Y. 10013

Maria J. Gonzalez
7516 N. Shepshead Rd.
Brooklyn, N.Y. 11240

Leslie B. Brautenwieler
21-75A Seiler Terr.
Flushing, N.J. 11367

1.____

2.____

3.____

4.____

5.____

2 (#2)

COLUMN I	COLUMN II	
6. Rigoberto J. Peredes 157 Twin Towers, #18F Tottenville, S. I., N.Y,	Rigoberto J. Peredes 157 Twin Towers, #18F Tottenville, S.I., N.Y.	6.____
7. Pietro F. Albino P.O. Box 7548 Floral Park, N.Y. 11005	Pietro F. Albina P.O. Box 7458 Floral Park, N.Y. 11005	7.____
8. Joanne Zimmerman Bldg. SW, Room 314 532-4601	Joanne Zimmermann Bldg. SW, Room 314 532-4601	8.____
9. Carlyle Whetstone Payroll Div. –A, Room 212A 262-5000, ext. 471	Carlyle Whetstone Payroll Div. –A, Room 212A 262-5000, ext. 417	9.____
10. Kenneth Chiang Legal Council, Room 9745 (201) 416-9100, ext. 17	Kenneth Chiang Legal Counsel, Room 9745 (201) 416-9100, Ext. 17	10.____
11. Ethel Koenig Personnel Services Division, Room 433; 635-7572	Ethel Hoenig Personal Services Division, Room 433; 635-7527	11.____
12. Joyce Ehrhardt Office of the Administrator, Room W56; 387-8706	Joyce Ehrhart Office of the Administrator, Room W56; 387-7806	12.____
13. Ruth Lang EAM Bldg., Room C101 625-2000, ext. 765	Ruth Lang EAM Bldg., Room C110 625-2000, ext. 765	13.____
14. Anne Marie Ionozzi Investigations, Room 827 576-4000, ext. 832	Anna Marie Ionozzi Investigation, Room 827 566-4000, ext. 832	14.____
15. Willard Jameson Fm C Bldg., Room 687 454-3010	Willard Jamieson Fm C Bldg., Room 687 454-3010	15.____

KEY (CORRECT ANSWERS)

1. B
2. D
3. A
4. A
5. C
6. D
7. B
8. D
9. B
10. A
11. C
12. B
13. A
14. C
15. A

TEST 3

DIRECTIONS: Questions 1 through 10 are to be answered on the basis of the following instructions. *PRINT THE LETTER OF THE CORRECT ANSWER IN THE SPACE AT THE RIGHT.*

INSTRUCTIONS
For each such set of names, addresses, and numbers listed in Columns I and II, select your answer from the following options:
- The names in Columns I and II are different,
- The addresses in Columns I and II are different,
- The numbers in Columns I and II are different,
- The names, addresses, and numbers in Columns I and II are identical.

	COLUMN I	COLUMN II	
1.	Francis Jones 62 Stately Avenue 96-12446	Francis Jones 62 Stately Avenue 96-21446	1.____
2.	Julio Montez 19 Ponderosa Road 56-73161	Julio Montez 19 Ponderosa Road 56-71361	2.____
3.	Mary Mitchell 2314 Melbourne Drive 68-92172	Mary Mitchell 2314 Melbourne Drive 68-92172	3.____
4.	Harry Patterson 25 Dunne Street 14-33430	Harry Patterson 25 Dunne Street 14-34330	4.____
5.	Patrick Murphy 171 West Hosmer Street 93-81214	Patrick Murphy 171 West Hosmer Street 93-18214	5.____
6.	August Schultz 816 St. Clair Avenue 53-40149	August Schultz 816 St. Claire Avenue 53-40149	6.____
7.	George Taft 72 Runnymede Street 47-04033	George Taft 72 Runnymede Street 47-04023	7.____
8.	Angus Henderson 1418 Madison Street 81-76375	Angus Henderson 1318 Madison Street 81-76375	8.____

2 (#3)

COLUMN I	COLUMN II	
9. Carolyn Mazur 12 Riverview Road 38-99615	Carolyn Mazur 12 Rivervane Road 38-99615	9.____
10. Adele Russell 1725 Lansing Lane 72-91962	Adela Russell 1725 Lansing Lane 72-91962	10.____

KEY (CORRECT ANSWERS)

1.	C	6.	B
2.	C	7.	C
3.	D	8.	D
4.	C	9.	B
5.	C	10.	A

TEST 4

DIRECTIONS: Questions 1 through 20 test how good you are at catching mistakes in typing or printing. In each question, the name and address in Column II should be an exact copy of the name and address in Column I. Mark your answer
   A. If there is no mistake in either name or address;
   B. If there is a mistake in both name and address;
   C. If there is a mistake only in the name;
   D. If there is a mistake only in the address.
PRINT THE LETTER OF THE CORRECT ANSWER IN THE SPACE AT THE RIGHT.

COLUMN I   COLUMN II

1. Milos Yanocek   Milos Yanocek   1.____
    33-60 14 Street   33-60 14 Street
    Long Island City, N.Y. 11011   Long Island City, N.Y. 11001

2. Alphonse Sabattelo   Alphonse Sabbattelo   2.____
    24 Minnetta Lane   24 Minetta Lane
    New York, N.Y. 10006   New York, N.Y. 10006

3. Helen Steam   Helene Stearn   3.____
    5 Metropolitan Oval   5 Metropolitan Oval
    Bronx, N.Y. 10462   Bronx, N.Y. 10462

4. Jacob Weisman   Jacob Weisman   4.____
    231 Francis Lewis Boulevard   231 Francis Lewis Boulevard
    Forest Hills, N.Y. 11325   Forest Hills, N.Y. 11325

5. Riccardo Fuente   Riccardo Fuentes   5.____
    134 West 83 Street   134 West 88 Street
    New York, N.Y. 10024   New York, N.Y. 10024

6. Dennis Lauber   Dennis Lauder   6.____
    52 Avenue D   52 Avenue D
    Brooklyn, N.Y. 11216   Brooklyn, N.Y. 11216

7. Paul Cutter   Paul Cutter   7.____
    195 Galloway Avenue   175 Galloway Avenue
    Staten Island, N.Y. 10356   Staten Island, N.Y. 10365

8. Sean Donnelly   Sean Donnelly   8.____
    45-58 41 Avenue   45-58 41 Avenue
    Woodside, N.Y. 11168   Woodside, N.Y. 11168

9. Clyde Willot   Clyde Willat   9.____
    1483 Rockaway Avenue   1483 Rockaway Avenue
    Brooklyn, N.Y. 11238   Brooklyn, N.Y. 11238

2 (#4)

COLUMN I	COLUMN II	
10. Michael Stanakis 419 Sheriden Avenue Staten Island, N.Y. 10363	Michael Stanakis 419 Sheraden Avenue Staten Island, N.Y. 10363	10.____
11. Joseph DiSilva 63-84 Saunders Road Rego Park, N.Y. 11431	Joseph Disilva 64-83 Saunders Road Rego Park, N.Y. 11431	11.____
12. Linda Polansky 2224 Fendon Avenue Bronx, N.Y. 20464	Linda Polansky 2255 Fenton Avenue Bronx, N.Y. 10464	12.____
13. Alfred Klein 260 Hillside Terrace Staten Island, N.Y. 15545	Alfred Klein 260 Hillside Terrace Staten Island, N.Y. 15545	13.____
14. William McDonnell 504 E. 55 Street New York, N.Y. 10103	William McConnell 504 E. 55 Street New York, N.Y. 10108	14.____
15. Angela Cipolla 41-11 Parson Avenue Flushing, N.Y. 11446	Angela Cipola 41-11 Parsons Avenue Flushing, N.Y. 11446	15.____
16. Julie Sheridan 1212 Ocean Avenue Brooklyn, N.Y. 11237	Julia Sheridan 1212 Ocean Avenue Brooklyn, N.Y. 11237	16.____
17. Arturo Rodriguez 2156 Cruger Avenue Bronx, N.Y. 10446	Arturo Rodrigues 2156 Cruger Avenue Bronx, N.Y. 10446	17.____
18. Helen McCabe 2044 East 19 Street Brooklyn, N.Y. 11204	Helen McCabe 2040 East 19 Street Brooklyn, N.Y. 11204	18.____
19. Charles Martin 526 West 160 Street New York, N.Y. 10022	Charles Martin 526 West 160 Street New York, N.Y. 10022	19.____
20. Morris Rabinowitz 31 Avenue M Brooklyn, N.Y. 11216	Morris Rabinowitz 31 Avenue N Brooklyn, N.Y. 11216	20.____

KEY (CORRECT ANSWERS)

1.	D	11.	B
2.	B	12.	D
3.	C	13.	A
4.	A	14.	B
5.	B	15.	B
6.	C	16.	C
7.	D	17.	C
8.	A	18.	D
9.	B	19.	A
10.	D	20.	D

TEST 5

DIRECTIONS: In copying the addresses below from Column A to the same line in Column B, an Agent-in-Training made some errors. For Questions 1 through 5, if you find that the agent made an error in
only one line, mark your answer A;
only two lines, mark your answer B;
only three lines, mark your answer C;
all four lines, mark your answer D.

EXAMPLE

COLUMN A	COLUMN B
24 Third Avenue	24 Third Avenue
5 Lincoln Road	5 Lincoln Street
50 Central Park West	6 Central Park West
37-21 Queens Boulevard	21-37 Queens Boulevard

Since errors were made on only three lines, namely the second, third, and fourth, the CORRECT answer is C.
PRINT THE LETTER OF THE CORRECT ANSWER IN THE SPACE AT THE RIGHT.

	COLUMN A	COLUMN B	
1.	57-22 Springfield Boulevard 94 Gun Hill Road 8 New Dorp Lane 36 Bedford Avenue	75-22 Springfield Boulevard 94 Gun Hill Avenue 8 New Drop Lane 36 Bedford Avenue	1.____
2.	538 Castle Hill Avenue 54-15 Beach Channel Drive 21 Ralph Avenue 162 Madison Avenue	538 Castle Hill Avenue 54-15 Beach Channel Drive 21 Ralph Avenue 162 Morrison Avenue	2.____
3.	49 Thomas Street 27-21 Northern Blvd. 86 125th Street 872 Atlantic Ave.	49 Thomas Street 21-27 Northern Blvd. 86 125th Street 872 Baltic Ave,	3.____
4.	261-17 Horace Harding Expwy. 191 Fordham Road 6 Victory Blvd. 552 Oceanic Ave.	261-17 Horace Harding Pkwy. 191 Fordham Road 6 Victoria Blvd. 552 Ocean Ave.	4.____
5.	90-05 38th Avenue 19 Central Park West 9281 Avenue X 22 West Farms Square	90-05 36th Avenue 19 Central Park East 9281 Avenue X 22 West Farms Square	5.____

KEY (CORRECT ANSWERS)

1. C
2. A
3. B
4. C
5. B

TEST 6

DIRECTIONS: For Questions 1 through 10, choose the letter in Column II next to the number which EXACTLY matches the number in Column I. *PRINT THE LETTER OF THE CORRECT ANSWER IN THE SPACE AT THE RIGHT.*

<u>COLUMN I</u>   <u>COLUMN II</u>

1. 14235
   - A. 13254
   - B. 12435
   - C. 13245
   - D. 14235

   1.____

2. 70698
   - A. 90768
   - B. 60978
   - C. 70698]
   - D. 70968

   2.____

3. 11698
   - A. 11689
   - B. 11986
   - C. 11968
   - D. 11698

   3.____

4. 50497
   - A. 50947
   - B. 50497
   - C. 50749
   - D. 54097

   4.____

5. 69635
   - A. 60653
   - B. 69630
   - C. 69365
   - D. 69635

   5.____

6. 1201022011
   - A. 1201022011
   - B. 1201020211
   - C. 1202012011
   - D. 1021202011

   6.____

7. 3893981389
   - A. 3893891389
   - B. 3983981389
   - C. 3983891389
   - D. 3893981389

   7.____

8. 4765476589
   - A. 4765476598
   - B. 4765476588
   - C. 4765476589
   - D. 4765746589

   8.____

9. 8679678938
    A. 8679687938
    B. 8679678938
    C. 8697678938
    D. 8678678938

    9.____

10. 6834836932
    A. 6834386932
    B. 6834836923
    C. 6843836932
    D. 6834836932

    10.____

Questions 11-15.

DIRECTIONS: For Questions 11 through 15, determine how many of the symbols in Column Z are exactly the same as the symbol in Column Y.
If none is exactly the same, answer A;
If only one symbol is exactly the same, answer B;
If two symbols are exactly the same, answer C;
If three symbols are exactly the same, answer D.

COLUMN Y	COLUMN Z	
11. A123B1266	A123B1366 A123B1266 A133B1366 A123B1266	11.____
12. CC28D3377	CD22D3377 CC38D3377 CC28C3377 CC28D2277	12.____
13. M21AB201X	M12AB201X M21AB201X M21AB201Y M21BA201X	13.____
14. PA383Y744	AP383Y744 PA338Y744 PA388Y744 PA383Y774	14.____
15. PB2Y8893	PB2Y8893 PB2Y8893 PB3Y8898 PB2Y8893	15.____

KEY (CORRECT ANSWERS)

1.	D	6.	A	11.	C
2.	C	7.	D	12.	A
3.	D	8.	C	13.	B
4.	B	9.	B	14.	A
5.	D	10.	D	15.	D

NAME AND NUMBER COMPARISONS

COMMENTARY

This test seeks to measure your ability and disposition to do a job carefully and accurately, your attention to exactness and preciseness of detail, your alertness and versatility in discerning similarities and differences between things, and your power in systematically handling written language symbols.

It is actually a test of your ability to do academic and/or clerical work, using the basic elements of verbal (qualitative) and mathematical (quantitative) learning—words and numbers.

EXAMINATION SECTION

TEST 1

DIRECTIONS: In each line across the page there are three names or numbers that are much alike. Compare the three names or numbers and decide which ones are exactly alike. *PRINT IN THE SPACE AT THE RIGHT THE LETTER:*
A. if all THREE names or numbers are exactly alike
B. if only the FIRST and SECOND names or numbers are ALIKE
C. if only the FIRST and THIRD names or numbers are alike
D. if only the SECOND or THIRD names or numbers are alike
E. if ALL THREE names or numbers are DIFFERENT

1.	Davis Hazen	David Hozen	David Hazen	1.____
2.	Lois Appel	Lois Appel	Lois Apfel	2.____
3.	June Allan	Jane Allan	Jane Allan	3.____
4.	10235	10235	10235	4.____
5.	32614	32164	32614	5.____

TEST 2

1.	2395890	2395890	2395890	1.____
2.	1926341	1926347	1926314	2.____
3.	E. Owens McVey	E. Owen McVey	E. Owen McVay	3.____
4.	Emily Neal Rouse	Emily Neal Rowse	Emily Neal Rowse	4.____
5.	H. Merritt Audubon	H. Merriott Audubon	H. Merritt Audubon	5.____

TEST 3

1.	6219354	6219354	6219354	1.____
2.	231793	2312793	2312793	2.____
3.	1065407	1065407	1065047	3.____
4.	Francis Ransdell	Frances Ramsdell	Francis Ramsdell	4.____
5.	Cornelius Detwiler	Cornelius Detwiler	Cornelius Detwiler	5.____

TEST 4

1.	6452054	6452564	6542054	1.____
2.	8501268	8501268	8501286	2.____
3.	Ella Burk Newham	Ella Burk Newnham	Elena Burk Newnham	3.____
4.	Jno. K. Ravencroft	Jno. H. Ravencroft	Jno. H. Ravencoft	4.____
5.	Martin Wills Pullen	Martin Wills Pulen	Martin Wills Pullen	5.____

TEST 5

1.	3457988	3457986	3457986	1.____
2.	4695682	4695862	4695682	2.____
3.	Stricklund Kaneydy	Sticklund Kanedy	Stricklund Kanedy	3.____
4.	Joy Harlor Witner	Joy Harloe Witner	Joy Harloe Witner	4.____
5.	R.M.O. Uberroth	R.M.O. Uberroth	R.N.O. Uberroth	5.____

TEST 6

1.	1592514	1592574	1592574	1.____
2.	2010202	2010202	2010220	2.____
3.	6177396	6177936	6177396	3.____
4.	Drusilla S. Ridgeley	Drusilla S. Ridgeley	Drusilla S. Ridgeley	4.____
5.	Andrei I. Tooumantzev	Andrei I. Tourmantzev	Andrei I. Toumantzov	5.____

TEST 7

1.	5261383	5261383	5261338	1.____
2.	8125690	8126690	8125609	2.____
3.	W.E. Johnston	W.E. Johnson	W.E. Johnson	3.____
4.	Vergil L. Muller	Vergil L. Muller	Vergil L. Muller	4.____
5.	Atherton R. Warde	Asheton R. Warde	Atherton P. Warde	5.____

TEST 8

1.	013469.5	023469.5	02346.95	1.____
2.	33376	333766	333766	2.____
3.	Ling-Temco-Vought	Ling-Tenco-Vought	Ling-Temco Vought	3.____
4.	Lorilard Corp.	Lorillard Corp.	Lorrilard Corp.	4.____
5.	American Agronomics Corporation	American Agronomics Corporation	American Agronomic Corporation	5.____

TEST 9

1.	436592864	436592864	436592864	1.____
2.	197765123	197755123	197755123	2.____
3.	Dewaay Cortvriendt International S.A.	Deway Cortvriendt International S.A.	Deway Corturiendt International S.A.	3.____
4.	Crédit Lyonnais	Crèdit Lyonnais	Crèdit Lyonais	4.____
5.	Algemene Bank Nederland N.V.	Algamene Bank Nederland N.V.	Algemene Bank Naderland N.V.	5.____

TEST 10

1.	00032572	0.0032572	00032522	1.____
2.	399745	399745	398745	2.____
3.	Banca Privata Finanziaria S.p.A.	Banca Privata Finanzaria S.P.A.	Banca Privata Finanziaria S.P.A.	3.____
4.	Eastman Dillon, Union Securities & Co.	Eastman Dillon, Union Securities Co.	Eastman Dillon, Union Securities & Co.	4.____
5.	Arnhold and S. Bleichroeder, Inc.	Arnhold & S. Bleichroeder, Inc.	Arnold and S. Bleichroeder, Inc.	5.____

TEST 11

DIRECTIONS: Answer the questions below on the basis of the following instructions: For each such numbered set of names, addresses, and numbers listed in Columns I and II, select your answer from the following options:
  A. The names in Columns I and II are different
  B. The addresses in Columns I and II are different
  C. The numbers in Columns I and II are different
  D. The names, addresses and numbers are identical

1. Francis Jones   Francis Jones   1.____
    62 Stately Avenue   62 Stately Avenue
    96-12446   96-21446

2. Julio Montez   Julio Montez   2.____
    19 Ponderosa Road   19 Ponderosa Road
    56-73161   56-71361

3. Mary Mitchell   Mary Mitchell   3.____
    2314 Melbourne Drive   2314 Melbourne Drive
    68-92172   68-92172

4. Harry Patterson   Harry Patterson   4.____
    25 Dunne Street   25 Dunne Street
    14-33430   14-34330

5. Patrick Murphy   Patrick Murphy   5.____
    171 West Hosmer Street   171 West Hosmer Street
    93-81214   93-18214

TEST 12

1. August Schultz
816 St. Clair Avenue
53-40149

   August Schultz
816 St. Claire Avenue
53-40149

   1.____

2. George Taft
72 Runnymede Street
47-04033

   George Taft
72 Runnymede Street
47-04023

   2.____

3. Angus Henderson
1418 Madison Street
81-76375

   Angus Henderson
1418 Madison Street
81-76375

   3.____

4. Carolyn Mazur
12 Rivenlew Road
38-99615

   Carolyn Mazur
12 Rivervane Road
38-99615

   4.____

5. Adele Russell
1725 Lansing Lane
72-91962

   Adela Russell
1725 Lansing Lane
72-91962

   5.____

TEST 13

DIRECTIONS: The following questions are based on the instructions given below. In each of the following questions, the 3-line name and address in Column I is the master-list entry, and the 3-line entry in Column II is the information to be checked against the master list.
If there is one line that is NOT exactly alike, mark your answer A.
If there are two lines NOT exactly alike, mark your answer B.
If there are three lines NOT exactly alike, mark your answer C.
If the lines ALL are exactly alike, mark your answer D.

1. Jerome A. Jackson   Jerome A. Johnson   1.____
    1243 14th Avenue   1234 14th Avenue
    New York, N.Y. 10023   New York, N.Y. 10023

2. Sophie Strachtheim   Sophie Strachtheim   2.____
    33-28 Connecticut Ave.   33-28 Connecticut Ave.
    Far Rockaway, N.Y. 11697   Far Rockaway, N.Y. 11697

3. Elisabeth NT. Gorrell   Elizabeth NT. Correll   3.____
    256 Exchange St   256 Exchange St.
    New York, N.Y. 10013   New York, N.Y. 10013

4. Maria J. Gonzalez   Maria J. Gonzalez   4.____
    7516 E. Sheepshead Rd.   7516 N. Shepshead Rd.
    Brooklyn, N.Y. 11240   Brooklyn, N.Y. 11240

5. Leslie B. Brautenweiler   Leslie B. Brautenwieler   5.____
    21-57A Seller Terr.   21-75ASeiler Terr.
    Flushing, N.Y. 11367   Flushing, N.J. 11367

KEY (CORRECT ANSWERS)

TEST 1	TEST 2	TEST 3	TEST 4	TEST 5	TEST 6	TEST 7
1. E	1. A	1. A	1. E	1. D	1. D	1. B
2. B	2. E	2. A	2. B	2. C	2. B	2. E
3. D	3. E	3. B	3. E	3. E	3. C	3. D
4. A	4. D	4. E	4. E	4. D	4. A	4. A
5. C	5. C	5. A	5. C	5. B	5. E	5. E

TEST 8	TEST 9	TEST 10	TEST 11	TEST 12	TEST 13
1. E	1. A	1. E	1. C	1. B	1. B
2. D	2. D	2. B	2. C	2. C	2. D
3. E	3. E	3. E	3. D	3. D	3. A
4. E	4. E	4. C	4. C	4. B	4. A
5. B	5. E	5. E	5. C	5. A	5. C

NAME AND NUMBER COMPARISONS

COMMENTARY

This test seeks to measure your ability and disposition to do a job carefully and accurately, your attention to exactness and preciseness of detail, your alertness and versatility in discerning similarities and differences between things, and your power in systematically handling written language symbols.

It is actually a test of your ability to do academic and/or clerical work, using the basic elements of verbal (qualitative) and mathematical (quantitative) learning—words <u>and</u> numbers.

EXAMINATION SECTION

TEST 1

DIRECTIONS: Questions 1 through 6 consist of sets of names and addresses. In each question, the name and address in Column II should be an exact copy of the name and address in Column II. *PRINT IN THE SPACE AT THE RIGHT THE LETTER*
- A. if there is a mistake only in the name
- B. if there is a mistake only in the address
- C. if there is a mistake in both name and address
- D. If there is no mistake in either name or address

SAMPLE:
Michael Filbert
456 Reade Street
New York, N.Y. 10013

Michael Filbert
644 Reade Street
New York, N.Y. 10013

Since there is a mistake only in the address, the answer is B.

1. Esta Wong
141 West 68 St.
New York, N.Y. 10023

   Esta Wang
   141 West 68 St.
   New York, N.Y. 10023   1.____

2. Dr. Alberto Grosso
3475 12th Avenue
Brooklyn, N.Y. 11218

   Dr. Alberto Grosso
   3475 12th Avenue
   Brooklyn, N.Y. 11218   2.____

3. Mrs. Ruth Bortlas
482 Theresa Ct.
Far Rockaway, N.Y. 11691

   Ms. Ruth Bortias
   482 Theresa Ct.
   Far Rockaway, N.Y. 11169   3.____

4. Mr. and Mrs. Howard Fox
2301 Sedgwick Ave.
Bronx, N.Y. 10468

   Mr. and Mrs. Howard Fox
   231 Sedgwick Ave.
   Bronx, N.Y. 10468   4.____

5. Miss Marjorie Black
223 East 23 Street
New York, N.Y. 10010

   Miss Margorie Black
   223 East 23 Street
   New York, N.Y. 10010   5.____

2 (#1)

6. Michelle Herman   Michelle Hermann   6.____
   806 Valley Rd.   806 Valley Dr.
   Old Tappan, N.J. 07675   Old Tappan, N.J. 07675

   ⎯⎯⎯⎯⎯⎯⎯⎯⎯

KEY (CORRECT ANSWERS)

1. A
2. D
3. C
4. B
5. A
6. C

⎯⎯⎯⎯⎯⎯⎯⎯⎯

TEST 2

DIRECTIONS: Questions 1 through 6 consist of sets of names and addresses. In each question, the name and address in Column II should be an exact copy of the name and address in Column II. *PRINT IN THE SPACE AT THE RIGHT THE LETTER*
- A. if there is a mistake only in the name
- B. if there is a mistake only in the address
- C. if there is a mistake in both name and address
- D. If there is no mistake in either name or address

1. Ms. Joan Kelly
   313 Franklin Ave.
   Brooklyn, N.Y. 11202

   Ms. Joan Kielly
   318 Franklin Ave.
   Brooklyn, N.Y. 11202

   1.____

2. Mrs. Eileen Engel
   47-24 86 Road
   Queens, N.Y. 11122

   Mrs. Ellen Engel
   47-24 86 Road
   Queens, N.Y. 11122

   2.____

3. Marcia Michaels
   213 E. 81 St.
   New York, N.Y. 10012

   Marcia Michaels
   213 E. 81 St.
   New York, N.Y. 10012

   3.____

4. Rev. Edward J. Smyth
   1401 Brandeis Street
   San Francisco, Calif. 96201

   Rev. Edward J. Smyth
   1401 Brandies Street
   San Francisco, Calif. 96201

   4.____

5. Alicia Rodriguez
   24-68 81 St.
   Elmhurst, N.Y. 11122

   Alicia Rodriquez
   2468 81 St.
   Elmhurst, N.Y. 11122

   5.____

6. Ernest Eissemann
   21 Columbia St.
   New York, N.Y. 10007

   Ernest Eisermann
   21 Columbia St.
   New York, N.Y. 10007

   6.____

KEY (CORRECT ANSWERS)

1. C
2. A
3. D
4. B
5. C
6. A

TEST 3

DIRECTIONS: Questions 1 through 8 consist of names, locations, and telephone numbers. In each question, the name, location and number in Column II should be an exact copy of the name, location, and number in Column I. *PRINT IN THE SPACE AT THE RIGHT THE LETTER*
- A. if there is a mistake in one line only
- B. if there is a mistake in two lines only
- C. if there is a mistake in three lines only
- D. if there are no mistakes in any of the lines

1. Ruth Lang
   EAM Bldg., Room C101
   625-2000, ext. 765

   Ruth Lang
   EAM Bldg., Room C110
   625-2000, ext. 765

   1.____

2. Anne Marie Ionozzi
   Investigations, Room 827
   576-4000, ext. 832

   Anna Marie Ionozzi
   Investigation, Room 827
   566-4000, ext. 832

   2.____

3. Willard Jameson
   Fm C Bldg. Room 687
   454-3010

   Willard Jamieson
   Fm C Bldg. Room 687
   454-3010

   3.____

4. Joanne Zimmermann
   Bldg. SW, Room 314
   532-4601

   Joanne Zimmermann
   Bldg. SW, Room 314
   532-4601

   4.____

5. Carlyle Whetstone
   Payroll Division-A, Room 212A
   262-5000, ext. 471

   Caryle Whetstone
   Payroll Division-A, Room 212A
   262-5000, ext. 417

   5.____

6. Kenneth Chiang
   Legal Council, Room 9745
   (201) 416-9100, ext. 17

   Kenneth Chiang
   Legal Counsel, Room 9745
   (201) 416-9100, ext. 17

   6.____

7. Ethel Koenig
   Personnel Services Div, Rm 433
   635-7572

   Ethel Hoenig
   Personal Services Div, Rm 433
   635-7527

   7.____

8. Joyce Ehrhardt
   Office of Administrator, Rm W56
   387-8706

   Joyce Ehrhart
   Office of Administrator, Rm W56
   387-7806

   8.____

KEY (CORRECT ANSWERS)

1. A
2. C
3. A
4. D
5. B
6. A
7. C
8. B

TEST 4

DIRECTIONS: Each of Questions 1 through 10 gives the identification number and name of a person who has received treatment at a certain hospital. You are to choose the option (A, B, C, or D) which has EXACTLY the same number and name as those given in the question.

SAMPLE QUESTION:
123765 Frank Y. Jones
  A. 123675 Frank Y. Jones
  B. 123765 Frank T. Jones
  C. 123765 Frank Y. Jones
  D. 123765 Frank Y. Jones

The correct answer is D, because it is the only option showing the identification number and name exactly as they are in the sample question.

1.   754898 Diane Malloy
    A. 745898 Diane Malloy   B. 754898 Dion Malloy
    C. 754898 Diane Malloy   D. 754898 Diane Maloy

2.   661818 Ferdinand Figueroa
    A. 661818 Ferdinand Figeuroa   B. 661618 Ferdinand Figueroa
    C. 661818 Ferdnand Figueroa   D. 661818 Ferdinand Figueroa

3.   100101 Norman D. Braustein
    A. 100101 Norman D. Braustein   B. 101001 Norman D. Braustein
    C. 100101 Norman P. Braustien   D. 100101 Norman D. Bruastein

4.   838696 Robert Kittredge
    A. 838969 Robert Kittredge   B. 838696 Robert Kittredge
    C. 388696 Robert Kittredge   D. 838696 Robert Kittridge

5.   243716 Abraham Soletsky
    A. 243716 Abrahm Soletsky   B. 243716 Abraham Solestky
    C. 243176 Abraham Soletsky   D. 243716 Abraham Soletsky

6.   981121 Phillip M. Maas
    A. 981121 Phillip M. Mass   B. 981211 Phillip M. Maas
    C. 981121 Phillip M. Maas   D. 981121 Phillip N. Maas

7.   786556 George Macalusso
    A. 785656 George Macalusso   B. 786556 George Macalusso
    C. 786556 George Maculusso   D. 786556 George Macluasso

8.   639472 Eugene Weber
    A. 639472 Eugene Weber   B. 639472 Eugene Webre
    C. 693472 Eugene Weber   D. 639742 Eugene Weber

2 (#4)

9. 724936 John J. Lomonaco							9._____
    A. 724936 John J. Lomanoco		B. 724396 John L. Lomonaco
    C. 7224936 John J. Lomonaco		D. 724936 John J. Lamonaco

10. 899868 Michael Schnitzer							10._____
    A. 899868 Micheal Schnitzer		B. 898968 Michael Schnizter
    C. 899688 Michael Schnitzer		D. 899868 Michael Schnitzer

KEY (CORRECT ANSWERS)

1.	C	6.	C
2.	D	7.	B
3.	A	8.	A
4.	B	9.	C
5.	D	10.	D

MEMORY FOR ADDRESSES

COMMENTARY

This is a test of your ability to learn a scheme, a system, a method, a procedure, or a routine during your training period.

More importantly, it is a test of your keenness of observation, your accuracy in noting details, and your acuteness of memory.

It is a test of your aptitude to learn.

DESCRIPTION OF THE TEST
In this test you will be given 25 addresses to remember. The addresses are divided into five groups. Each group of five addresses is in a box such as those below. Each box has a letter -- A,B,C,D,or E. You will have to learn which letter goes with each address. You will be given time to study in the examination room. In order to practice for this test, you need to be timed.

While you are doing the practice test, find out what is the best way for you to memorize which letter goes with each address. Some people learn best by studying the addresses in one box; then covering it and seeing whether they can say the addresses to themselves. If they can say them, they then try to learn the next box. If they cannot, they study the names in the first box again, and then try to say the names with the box covered. They do this for all the boxes. Other people learn best by studying across the page. Still others do best by memorizing everything at once. If you do not know your best way, try different ways and see which one is best for you. Do not try to memorize the names by writing them down because you won't be allowed to write them in the official examination.

HINTS FOR MEMORY FOR ADDRESSES TEST
* Be sure to spend the study period studying.
* Be sure to try to learn which letter goes with each address. It is to your advantage to learn as many as you can.
* Do not spend too much time on any one question.
* Do not get nervous about the time limit. (In the official test no one is expected to do all the questions in the time allowed.)
* If you are not sure of an answer, guess.

PART I

Sample Questions for Memory for Addresses

In this test you will have five boxes labeled A, B, C, D, and E. Each box contains five addresses. Three of the five are groups of street addresses like 1700–2599 Wood, 8500–8699 Lang, and 6200–6399 James, and two are names of places. They are different in each box.

You will also be given two lists of names. You will have to decide which box each name belongs in. When you are working on the first list, you will have the boxes with the names in front of you. When you are working on the second list, you will not be able to look at the boxes.

The addresses you will use for the Practice Test are given in the boxes below.

A	B	C	D	E
1700–2599 Wood Dushore 8500–8699 Lang Lott 6200–6399 James	2700–3299 Wood Jeriel 8700–9399 Lang Vanna 5700–6199 James	1300–1699 Wood Levering 9400–9499 Lang Ekron 6400–6499 James	3300–3599 Wood Bair 8000–8499 Lang Viborg 5000–5699 James	2600–2699 Wood Danby 9500–9999 Lang Lycan 4700–4999 James

Questions 1 through 5 show the way the questions look. You have to decide in which lettered box (A, B, C, D, or E) the address belongs and then mark that answer on the Sample Answer Sheet on this page.

1. Levering

    This address is in box C. So darken box C on the Sample Answer Sheet.

2. 2700–3299 Wood

    This address is in box B. So darken box B on the Sample Answer Sheet.

3. Vanna

    This address is in box B. So darken box B on the Sample Answer Sheet.

Now, you do questions 4 and 5.

4. 6200–6399 James

5. Bair

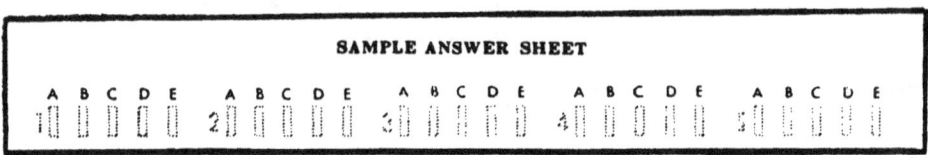

The answers for samples 4 and 5 are 4A and 5D.

Your practice test starts on the next page.

MEMORY FOR ADDRESSES -- PRACTICE TEST

STUDY -- 3 minutes

Now turn back to the Sample Questions above and spend 3 minutes memorizing the addresses in the boxes. TRY TO LEARN THE LOCATION OF AS MANY ADDRESSES AS YOU CAN. Cover each box with your hand and see if you can repeat, to yourself, the addresses in that box.

When the 3 minutes for studying are up, turn to page 3 and continue with the practice.

List 1

WORK—*3 minutes*

For each question, mark Sample Answer Sheet A on p. 5 to show the letter of the box in which the address belongs. Try to remember the location of as many addresses as you can. If you are not sure of an address, guess. Work only 3 minutes.

A	B	C	D	E
1700–2599 Wood Dushore 8500–8699 Lang Lott 6200–6399 James	2700–3299 Wood Jeriel 8700–9399 Lang Vanna 5700–6199 James	1300–1699 Wood Levering 9400–9499 Lang Ekron 6400–6499 James	3300–3599 Wood Bair 8000–8499 Lang Viborg 5000–5699 James	2600–2699 Wood Danby 9500–9999 Lang Lycan 4700–4999 James

 1. 6200–6399 James
 2. 1700–2599 Wood
 3. Bair
 4. 1700–2599 Wood
 5. Ekron
 6. Viborg
 7. Danby
 8. 8500–8699 Lang

 9. Lycan
10. 8000–8499 Lang
11. 4700–4999 James
12. 9400–9499 Lang
13. 2700–3299 Wood
14. Jeriel
15. 9500–9999 Lang
16. 1300–1699 Wood

17. 8700–9399 Lang
18. Levering
19. Vanna
20. 6400–6499 James
21. 3300–3599 Wood
22. Dushore
23. Lycan
24. 5700–6199 James

25. Lott
26. Viborg
27. Jeriel
28. 5000–5699 James
29. 2600–2699 Wood
30. 4700–4999 James
31. 2700–3299 Wood
32. 8000–8499 Lang

33. Ekron
34. 3300–3599 Wood
35. 9400–9499 Lang
36. 6200–6399 James
37. 2600–2699 Wood
38. 8500–8699 Lang
39. Levering
40. Lott

41. Bair
42. 1700–2599 Wood
43. 6400–6499 James
44. 9500–9999 Lang
45. Jeriel
46. 4700–4999 James
47. Dushore
48. Lycan

49. 1700–2599 Wood
50. 6200–6399 James
51. Vanna
52. Ekron
53. 8700–9399 Lang
54. Bair
55. 2600–2699 Wood
56. Dushore

57. 5700–6199 James
58. 1300–1699 Wood
59. Levering
60. Lott
61. Jeriel
62. 2600–2699 Wood
63. Lott
64. 4700–4999 James

65. Dushore
66. Danby
67. 8500–8699 Lang
68. Vanna
69. 2700–3299 Wood
70. 9500–9999 Lang
71. Viborg
72. Ekron

73. 6200–6399 James
74. 2600–2699 Wood
75. Levering
76. Lott
77. 1300–1699 Wood
78. Bair
79. Lycan
80. 5700–6199 James

81. Levering
82. 8700–9399 Lang
83. 5000–5699 James
84. 1700–2599 Wood
85. Jeriel
86. 6200–6399 James
87. Ekron
88. 2700–3299 Wood

STOP.

If you finish before the 3 minutes are up, go back and check your answers for the questions on this page for the rest of the 3 minutes.

When the 3 minutes are up, go on to page 4.

List 2

WORK—*3 minutes*

Now do these questions without looking back at the boxes with the addresses in them.

For each question, mark your answer on Sample Answer Sheet B on p. 5. If you are not sure of an answer, guess.

1. Jeriel
2. Dushore
3. 5000–5699 James
4. 1300–1699 Wood
5. 8500–8699 Lang
6. Bair
7. 5700–6199 James
8. Levering

9. Danby
10. Viborg
11. 8000–8499 Lang
12. 2700–3299 Wood
13. 9400–9499 Lang
14. 3300–3599 Wood
15. 4700–4999 James
16. 9500–9999 Lang

17. Ekron
18. 1300–1699 Wood
19. Vanna
20. Lycan
21. 8700–9399 Lang
22. Dushore
23. 6200–6399 James
24. Lott

25. 2700–3299 Wood
26. 5700–6199 James
27. Levering
28. 9500–9999 Lang
29. 2600–2699 Wood
30. 3300–3599 Wood
31. Viborg
32. 9400–9499 Lang

33. Jeriel
34. Bair
35. 8500–8699 Lang
36. 1700–2599 Wood
37. 8000–8499 Lang
38. Danby
39. Ekron
40. 4700–4999 James

41. Dushore
42. Vanna
43. 5000–5699 James
44. Lott
45. 1300–1699 Wood
46. Levering
47. 5700–6199 James
48. 9500–9999 Lang

49. Bair
50. 8700–9399 Lang
51. 6200–6399 James
52. 9400–9499 Lang
53. Viborg
54. 8000–8499 Lang
55. 4700–4999 James
56. Lycan

57. Vanna
58. Danby
59. 5700–6199 James
60. Lott
61. 2700–3299 Wood
62. 5000–5699 James
63. 1700–2599 Wood
64. 8000–8499 Lang

65. 9400–9499 Lang
66. Jeriel
67. 9500–9999 Lang
68. Dushore
69. 2600–2699 Wood
70. 8500–8699 Lang
71. Levering
72. 5000–5699 James

73. Dushore
74. 8000–8499 Lang
75. Bair
76. Ekron
77. 6200–6399 James
78. 3300–3599 Wood
79. 8700–9399 Lang
80. Viborg

81. 4700–4999 James
82. Lycan
83. 1700–2599 Wood
84. 8500–8699 Lang
85. 1300–1699 Wood
86. Jeriel
87. Danby
88. 6400–6499 James

STOP.

If you finish before the end of 3 minutes, go back and be sure that you are satisfied with your answers.

Second Study

STUDY—*5 minutes*

You can see that memory is important in this test.

Now turn back to page 2 and spend 5 minutes memorizing the addresses in the boxes. TRY TO MEMORIZE THE LOCATION OF AS MANY ADDRESSES AS YOU CAN. Cover each box with your hand and see if you can repeat, to yourself, the addresses in that box.

When the 5 minutes for studying are up, turn to page 6 and continue with the practice.

SAMPLE ANSWER SHEET A

1 A B C D E	2 A B C D E	3 A B C D E	4 A B C D E	5 A B C D E	6 A B C D E	7 A B C D E	8 A B C D E
9 A B C D E	10 A B C D E	11 A B C D E	12 A B C D E	13 A B C D E	14 A B C D E	15 A B C D E	16 A B C D E
17 A B C D E	18 A B C D E	19 A B C D E	20 A B C D E	21 A B C D E	22 A B C D E	23 A B C D E	24 A B C D E
25 A B C D E	26 A B C D E	27 A B C D E	28 A B C D E	29 A B C D E	30 A B C D E	31 A B C D E	32 A B C D E
33 A B C D E	34 A B C D E	35 A B C D E	36 A B C D E	37 A B C D E	38 A B C D E	39 A B C D E	40 A B C D E
41 A B C D E	42 A B C D E	43 A B C D E	44 A B C D E	45 A B C D E	46 A B C D E	47 A B C D E	48 A B C D E
49 A B C D E	50 A B C D E	51 A B C D E	52 A B C D E	53 A B C D E	54 A B C D E	55 A B C D E	56 A B C D E
57 A B C D E	58 A B C D E	59 A B C D E	60 A B C D E	61 A B C D E	62 A B C D E	63 A B C D E	64 A B C D E
65 A B C D E	66 A B C D E	67 A B C D E	68 A B C D E	69 A B C D E	70 A B C D E	71 A B C D E	72 A B C D E
73 A B C D E	74 A B C D E	75 A B C D E	76 A B C D E	77 A B C D E	78 A B C D E	79 A B C D E	80 A B C D E
81 A B C D E	82 A B C D E	83 A B C D E	84 A B C D E	85 A B C D E	86 A B C D E	87 A B C D E	88 A B C D E

SAMPLE ANSWER SHEET B

1 A B C D E	2 A B C D E	3 A B C D E	4 A B C D E	5 A B C D E	6 A B C D E	7 A B C D E	8 A B C D E
9 A B C D E	10 A B C D E	11 A B C D E	12 A B C D E	13 A B C D E	14 A B C D E	15 A B C D E	16 A B C D E
17 A B C D E	18 A B C D E	19 A B C D E	20 A B C D E	21 A B C D E	22 A B C D E	23 A B C D E	24 A B C D E
25 A B C D E	26 A B C D E	27 A B C D E	28 A B C D E	29 A B C D E	30 A B C D E	31 A B C D E	32 A B C D E
33 A B C D E	34 A B C D E	35 A B C D E	36 A B C D E	37 A B C D E	38 A B C D E	39 A B C D E	40 A B C D E
41 A B C D E	42 A B C D E	43 A B C D E	44 A B C D E	45 A B C D E	46 A B C D E	47 A B C D E	48 A B C D E
49 A B C D E	50 A B C D E	51 A B C D E	52 A B C D E	53 A B C D E	54 A B C D E	55 A B C D E	56 A B C D E
57 A B C D E	58 A B C D E	59 A B C D E	60 A B C D E	61 A B C D E	62 A B C D E	63 A B C D E	64 A B C D E
65 A B C D E	66 A B C D E	67 A B C D E	68 A B C D E	69 A B C D E	70 A B C D E	71 A B C D E	72 A B C D E
73 A B C D E	74 A B C D E	75 A B C D E	76 A B C D E	77 A B C D E	78 A B C D E	79 A B C D E	80 A B C D E
81 A B C D E	82 A B C D E	83 A B C D E	84 A B C D E	85 A B C D E	86 A B C D E	87 A B C D E	88 A B C D E

SAMPLE ANSWER SHEET C

1 A B C D E	2 A B C D E	3 A B C D E	4 A B C D E	5 A B C D E	6 A B C D E	7 A B C D E	8 A B C D E
9 A B C D E	10 A B C D E	11 A B C D E	12 A B C D E	13 A B C D E	14 A B C D E	15 A B C D E	16 A B C D E
17 A B C D E	18 A B C D E	19 A B C D E	20 A B C D E	21 A B C D E	22 A B C D E	23 A B C D E	24 A B C D E
25 A B C D E	26 A B C D E	27 A B C D E	28 A B C D E	29 A B C D E	30 A B C D E	31 A B C D E	32 A B C D E
33 A B C D E	34 A B C D E	35 A B C D E	36 A B C D E	37 A B C D E	38 A B C D E	39 A B C D E	40 A B C D E
41 A B C D E	42 A B C D E	43 A B C D E	44 A B C D E	45 A B C D E	46 A B C D E	47 A B C D E	48 A B C D E
49 A B C D E	50 A B C D E	51 A B C D E	52 A B C D E	53 A B C D E	54 A B C D E	55 A B C D E	56 A B C D E
57 A B C D E	58 A B C D E	59 A B C D E	60 A B C D E	61 A B C D E	62 A B C D E	63 A B C D E	64 A B C D E
65 A B C D E	66 A B C D E	67 A B C D E	68 A B C D E	69 A B C D E	70 A B C D E	71 A B C D E	72 A B C D E
73 A B C D E	74 A B C D E	75 A B C D E	76 A B C D E	77 A B C D E	78 A B C D E	79 A B C D E	80 A B C D E
81 A B C D E	82 A B C D E	83 A B C D E	84 A B C D E	85 A B C D E	86 A B C D E	87 A B C D E	88 A B C D E

List 1—Second Time

WORK—5 minutes

For each question, mark your answer on **Sample Answer Sheet C** on p.5. Try to remember the location of as many addresses as you can.

A	B	C	D	E
1700–2599 Wood Dushore 8500–8699 Lang Lott 6200–6399 James	2700–3299 Wood Jeriel 8700–9399 Lang Vanna 5700–6199 James	1300–1699 Wood Levering 9400–9499 Lang Ekron 6400–6499 James	3300–3599 Wood Bair 8000–8499 Lang Viborg 5000–5699 James	2600–2699 Wood Danby 9500–9999 Lang Lycan 4700–4999 James

1. 6200–6399 James
2. 1700–2599 Wood
3. Bair
4. 1700–2599 Wood
5. Ekron
6. Viborg
7. Danby
8. 8500–8699 Lang

9. Lycan
10. 8000–8499 Lang
11. 4700–4999 James
12. 9400–9499 Lang
13. 2700–3299 Wood
14. Jeriel
15. 9500–9999 Lang
16. 1300–1699 Wood

17. 8700–9399 Lang
18. Levering
19. Vanna
20. 6400–6499 James
21. 3300–3599 Wood
22. Dushore
23. Lycan
24. 5700–6199 James

25. Lott
26. Viborg
27. Jeriel
28. 5000–5699 James
29. 2600–2699 Wood
30. 4700–4999 James
31. 2700–3299 Wood
32. 8000–8499 Lang

33. Ekron
34. 3300–3599 Wood
35. 9400–9499 Lang
36. 6200–6399 James
37. 2600–2699 Wood
38. 8500–8699 Lang
39. Levering
40. Lott

41. Bair
42. 1700–2599 Wood
43. 6400–6499 James
44. 9500–9999 Lang
45. Jeriel
46. 4700–4999 James
47. Dushore
48. Lycan

49. 1700–2599 Wood
50. 6200–6399 James
51. Vanna
52. Ekron
53. 8700–9399 Lang
54. Bair
55. 2600–2699 Wood
56. Dushore

57. 5700–6199 James
58. 1300–1699 Wood
59. Levering
60. Lott
61. Jeriel
62. 2600–2699 Wood
63. Lott
64. 4700–4999 James

65. Dushore
66. Danby
67. 8500–8699 Lang
68. Vanna
69. 2700–3299 Wood
70. 9500–9999 Lang
71. Viborg
72. Ekron

73. 6200–6399 James
74. 2600–2699 Wood
75. Levering
76. Lott
77. 1300–1699 Wood
78. Bair
79. Lycan
80. 5700–6199 James

81. Levering
82. 8700–9399 Lang
83. 5000–5699 James
84. 1700–2599 Wood
85. Jeriel
86. 6200–6399 James
87. Ekron
88. 2700–3299 Wood

STOP.

If you finish before the 5 minutes are up, go back and check your answers for the questions on this page.

At the end of 5 minutes, turn to page 7.

List 2—Second Time

WORK—*5 minutes*

This is the section that counts. The other times were to help you learn the addresses.

Do these questions without looking back at the boxes with the addresses in them. Work for 5 minutes.

For each question, mark the Sample Answer Sheet on the next page to show the letter of the box in which the address belongs.

1. Jeriel	25. 2700–3299 Wood	49. Bair	73. Dushore
2. Dushore	26. 5700–6199 James	50. 8700–9399 Lang	74. 8000–8499 Lang
3. 5000–5699 James	27. Levering	51. 6200–6399 James	75. Bair
4. 1300–1699 Wood	28. 9500–9999 Lang	52. 9400–9499 Lang	76. Ekron
5. 8500–8699 Lang	29. 2600–2699 Wood	53. Viborg	77. 6200–6399 James
6. Bair	30. 3300–3599 Wood	54. 8000–8499 Lang	78. 3300–3599 Wood
7. 5700–6199 James	31. Viborg	55. 4700–4999 James	79. 8700–9399 Lang
8. Levering	32. 9400–9499 Lang	56. Lycan	80. Viborg
9. Danby	33. Jeriel	57. Vanna	81. 4700–4999 James
10. Viborg	34. Bair	58. Danby	82. Lycan
11. 8000–8499 Lang	35. 8500–8699 Lang	59. 5700–6199 James	83. 1700–2599 Wood
12. 2700–3299 Wood	36. 1700–2599 Wood	60. Lott	84. 8500–8699 Lang
13. 9400–9499 Lang	37. 8000–8499 Lang	61. 2700–3299 Wood	85. 1300–1699 Wood
14. 3300–3599 Wood	38. Danby	62. 5000–5699 James	86. Jeriel
15. 4700–4999 James	39. Ekron	63. 1700–2599 Wood	87. Danby
16. 9500–9999 Lang	40. 4700–4999 James	64. 8000–8499 Lang	88. 6400–6499 James
17. Ekron	41. Dushore	65. 9400–9499 Lang	
18. 1300–1699 Wood	42. Vanna	66. Jeriel	
19. Vanna	43. 5000–5699 James	67. 9500–9999 Lang	**STOP.**
20. Lycan	44. Lott	68. Dushore	
21. 8700–9399 Lang	45. 1300–1699 Wood	69. 2600–2699 Wood	If you finish before the
22. Dushore	46. Levering	70. 8500–8699 Lang	5 minutes are up, go back
23. 6200–6399 James	47. 5700–6199 James	71. Levering	and check your answers.
24. Lott	48. 9500–9999 Lang	72. 5000–5699 James	

At the end of the 5 minutes, compare your answers with those given in the Correct Answers for **sample questions on page** 8.

LIST 2 - SECOND TIME

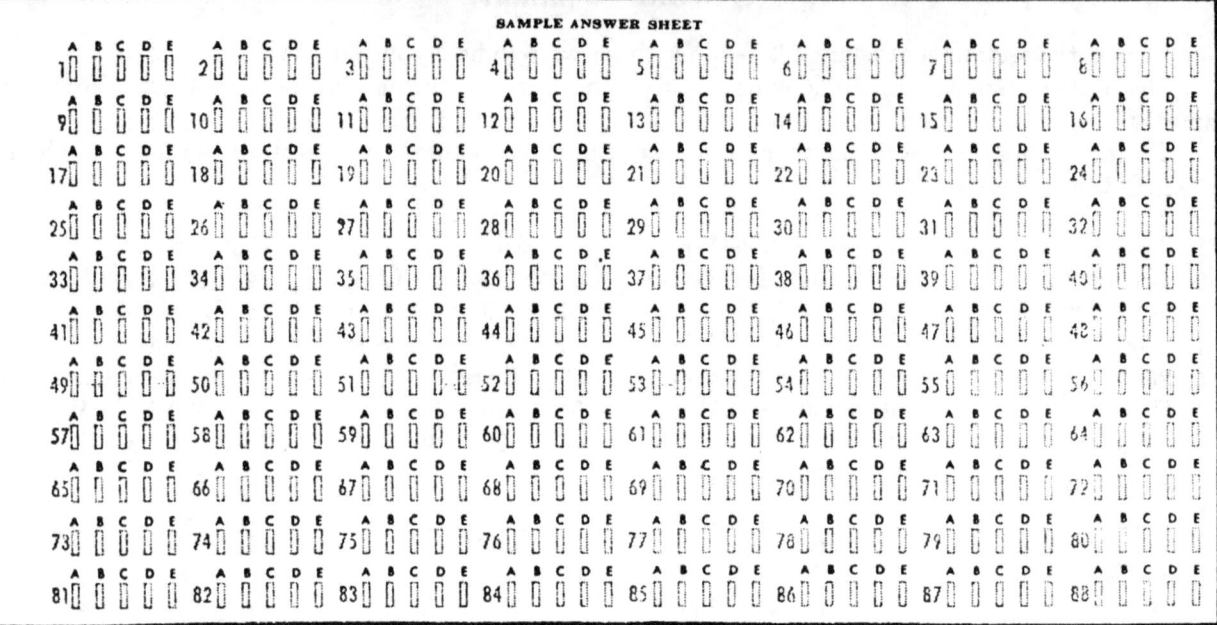

Now check your answers by comparing your answers with the correct answers shown below.

Count how many you got right, and write that number on this line ⟶ Number Right ____

Now count how many you got wrong, and write that number on this line ⟶ Number Wrong ____

Divide the Number Wrong by 4, and write the answer on this line ⟶ ¼ Number Wrong ____

Subtract the ¼ Number Wrong from the Number Right, and write the Difference on this line ⟶ Total Score ____

Meaning of Test Score
   If your Total Score is *44 or more*, you have a Good score.
   If your Total Score is from *26 to 43*, you have a Fair score.
   If your Total Score is *25 or less*, you are not doing too well.

You may be going too slowly, or you may be making too many mistakes. You need more practice.

PART II

Samples for Part II

Part II has five boxes labeled A, B, C, D, and E. Each box contains five addresses. Three of the five addresses are groups of street addresses like 2100–2799 Mall, 4800–4999 Cliff and 1900–2299 Laurel, and two are names of places. They are different in each box. You will be given two lists of addresses. For each street address or name in the list, you are to decide in which lettered box (A, B, C, D, or E) it belongs and then mark that box on the answer sheet. For List 1, the boxes will be shown on the same page with the addresses. While you are working on List 2, you will not be able to look at the boxes. Then you will have to match the addresses with the correct box from memory. Try to memorize the location of as many addresses as you can.

A	B	C	D	E
2100–2799 Mall Ceres 4800–4999 Cliff Natoma 1900–2299 Laurel	3900–4399 Mall Cedar 4000–4299 Cliff Foster 2300–2999 Laurel	4400–4599 Mall Niles 3300–3999 Cliff Dexter 3200–3799 Laurel	3400–3899 Mall Cicero 4500–4799 Cliff Pearl 3000–3199 Laurel	2800–3399 Mall Delhi 4300–4499 Cliff Magnet 1500–1899 Laurel

Sample Questions:

1. 3300–3999 Cliff—This address is in box C. So you would darken box C.
2. Natoma—This name is in box A. So you would darken box A.
3. Foster
4. 1500–1899 Laurel
5. 3900–4399 Mall
6. Pearl
7. 3200–3799 Laurel

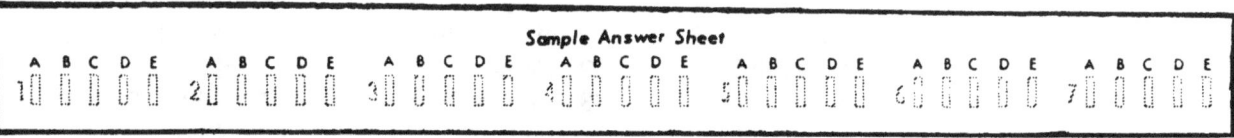

The answers to samples 3 to 7 are: 3B, 4E, 5B, 6D, and 7C.

In List 1 the boxes with the addresses will be before your eyes. Therefore you will be able to check your answers by looking at the top of the page. However, checking takes time and the more you remember, the faster you will be able to work. On List 2 the boxes with the addresses will *not* be shown. Then you will have only your memory to depend on when answering the questions. Thus, memory will be very important in this test.

Different people study in different ways. Many people find it easier to learn the addresses in one box at a time than to learn all the addresses at once.

You will now have *3 minutes* to study the addresses and letters so that you will have a good idea of the letter that goes with each address. Do not spend more than 3 minutes studying the addresses.

Now memorize the addresses in the boxes. These are the addresses that will be in the test. TRY TO LEARN THE LOCATION OF AS MANY ADDRESSES AS YOU CAN. Cover each box with your hand and see if you can repeat, to yourself, the addresses in that box.

DO NOT TURN THIS PAGE UNTIL THE TIME IS UP. THEN TURN TO PAGE 10.

List 1

For each question, mark the top answer sheet on the next page to show the letter of the box in which the address belongs. Try to remember the location of as many addresses as you can. You will now have *3 minutes* for List 1. If you are not sure of an answer you should guess.

A	B	C	D	E
2100–2799 Mall Ceres 4800–4999 Cliff Natoma 1900–2299 Laurel	3900–4399 Mall Cedar 4000–4299 Cliff Foster 2300–2999 Laurel	4400–4599 Mall Niles 3300–3999 Cliff Dexter 3200–3799 Laurel	3400–3899 Mall Cicero 4500–4799 Cliff Pearl 3000–3199 Laurel	2800–3399 Mall Delhi 4300–4499 Cliff Magnet 1500–1899 Laurel

1. Magnet
2. Niles
3. 3400–3899 Mall
4. 1900–2299 Laurel
5. Cicero
6. Dexter
7. 2300–2999 Laurel
8. 3300–3999 Cliff

9. 3200–3799 Laurel
10. 2100–2799 Mall
11. Pearl
12. 3200–3799 Laurel
13. Ceres
14. 4500–4799 Cliff
15. 3900–4399 Mall
16. Delhi

17. 4300–4499 Cliff
18. 3000–3199 Laurel
19. Ceres
20. Foster
21. Natoma
22. 4400–4599 Mall
23. Cedar
24. 2300–2999 Laurel

25. 1500–1899 Laurel
26. 4000–4299 Cliff
27. Dexter
28. Magnet
29. 3300–3999 Cliff
30. 3400–3899 Mall
31. Niles
32. 2100–2799 Mall

33. 1900–2299 Laurel
34. Cedar
35. Pearl
36. 2800–3399 Mall
37. 4800–4999 Cliff
38. 3900–4399 Mall
39. Foster
40. 3000–3199 Laurel

41. Ceres
42. Niles
43. 3400–3899 Mall
44. Delhi
45. 2300–2999 Laurel
46. 4500–4799 Cliff
47. Dexter
48. Magnet

49. 3300–3999 Cliff
50. Cicero
51. 4300–4499 Cliff
52. 3900–4399 Mall
53. Natoma
54. 3200–3799 Laurel
55. Pearl
56. 4000–4299 Cliff

57. 4500–4799 Cliff
58. 2100–2799 Mall
59. Foster
60. 4400–4599 Mall
61. 4800–4999 Cliff
62. Ceres
63. 2800–3399 Mall
64. 1500–1899 Laurel

65. Natoma
66. 3000–3199 Laurel
67. 4000–4299 Cliff
68. Niles
69. 2300–2999 Laurel
70. Magnet
71. Delhi
72. 4400–4599 Mall

73. Cicero
74. Cedar
75. 2800–3399 Mall
76. 1900–2299 Laurel
77. Dexter
78. Pearl
79. 4300–4499 Cliff
80. 3900–4399 Mall

81. Foster
82. 4800–4999 Cliff
83. Delhi
84. Ceres
85. 1500–1899 Laurel
86. Natoma
87. 2800–3399 Mall
88. Niles

STOP.

If you finish before the time is up, go back and check your answers for the questions on this page. Do not go to any other page until the time is up.

List 2

For each question, mark the answer sheet on the next page to show the letter of the box in which the address belongs. If you are not sure of an answer, you should guess. You will record your answers on the next page. While you are working on List 2, do not turn to any other page. You will have *3 minutes* to do this list.

1. Cedar
2. 4300–4499 Cliff
3. 4400–4599 Mall
4. Natoma
5. 2300–2999 Laurel
6. 4500–4799 Cliff
7. Ceres
8. 3400–3899 Mall

9. Delhi
10. Dexter
11. 1900–2299 Laurel
12. 3300–3999 Cliff
13. Cicero
14. 4000–4299 Cliff
15. 2100–2799 Mall
16. Foster

17. Magnet
18. Ceres
19. 2800–3399 Mall
20. 3200–3799 Laurel
21. 4300–4499 Cliff
22. Pearl
23. 3900–4399 Mall
24. Natoma

25. 4800–4999 Cliff
26. 1500–1899 Laurel
27. Cedar
28. 4400–4599 Mall
29. 4500–4799 Cliff
30. Dexter
31. 3000–3199 Laurel
32. Niles

33. Delhi
34. 3900–4399 Mall
35. Cicero
36. Dexter
37. 4800–4999 Cliff
38. 2300–2999 Laurel
39. 2100–2799 Mall
40. 3300–3999 Cliff

41. 3400–3899 Mall
42. 4300–4499 Cliff
43. Ceres
44. Foster
45. Magnet
46. 3200–3799 Laurel
47. Pearl
48. 1500–1899 Laurel

49. 4500–4799 Cliff
50. 1900–2299 Laurel
51. Niles
52. 3300–3999 Cliff
53. 2800–3399 Mall
54. Cicero
55. Delhi
56. 4000–4299 Cliff

57. Dexter
58. Magnet
59. 3000–3199 Laurel
60. 3900–4399 Mall
61. Natoma
62. 3000–3199 Laurel
63. 4300–4499 Cliff
64. Cedar

65. 4400–4599 Mall
66. 1500–1899 Laurel
67. 4800–4999 Cliff
68. Delhi
69. Pearl
70. 2300–2999 Laurel
71. 4500–4799 Cliff
72. Niles

73. 4000–4299 Cliff
74. 3400–3899 Mall
75. 1900–2299 Laurel
76. 2800–3399 Mall
77. Ceres
78. Magnet
79. Cicero
80. 3200–3799 Laurel

81. 3000–3199 Laurel
82. 3900–4399 Mall
83. Natoma
84. 3300–3999 Cliff
85. 3400–3899 Mall
86. Foster
87. 2100–2799 Mall
88. 4300–4499 Cliff

If you finish before the time is up, go back and check your answers to this part only. When the time is up turn back to page 9 and study the boxes again. You will have *5 minutes* to restudy the addresses. When that time is up, go on to page 10 and do that list again, using the bottom answer sheet on page 11. You will have *5 minutes* to do List 1 again. When that time is up turn to page 14 and read the instructions.

SAMPLE ANSWER SHEET

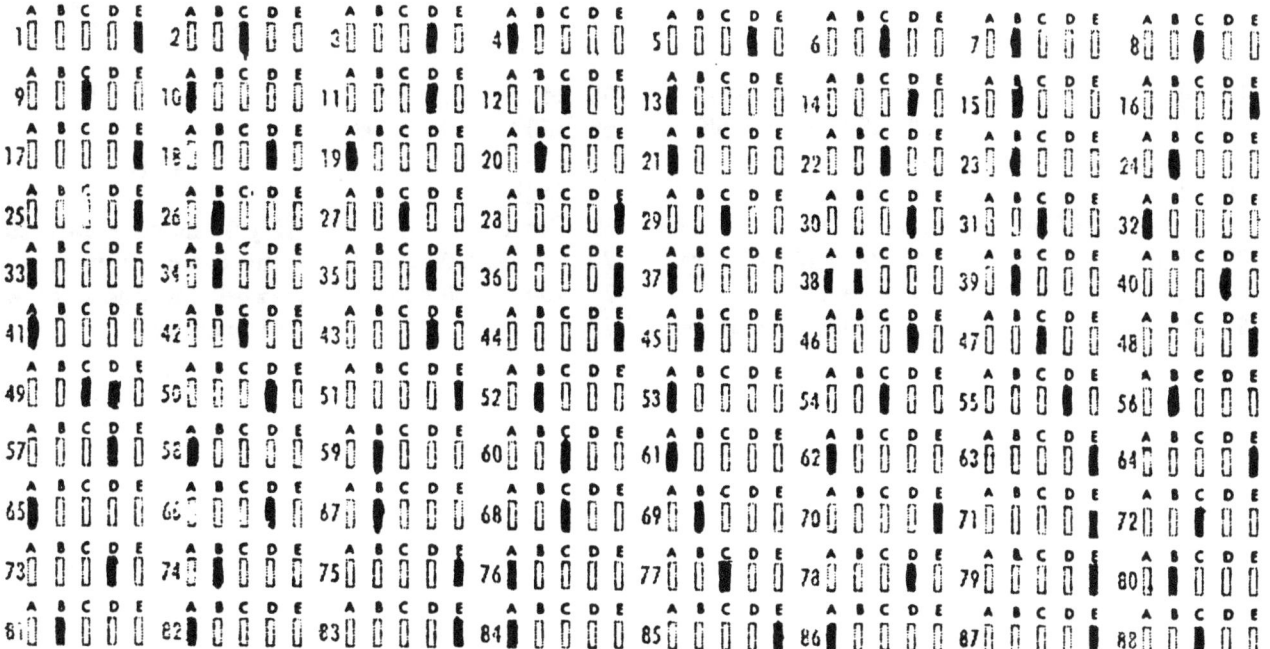

KEY (CORRECT ANSWERS)

LIST 1

Test-List 2

For each question, mark your answer sheet to show the letter of the box in which the address belongs. Use the Sample Answer Sheet on page 15. You will have *5 minutes* to do Test-List 2. During the 5 minutes for this list, do not turn to any other page.

Then compare your answers with those given in the Correct Answers for Test-List 2 on page 16.

1. Cedar
2. 4300–4499 Cliff
3. 4400–4599 Mall
4. Natoma
5. 2300–2999 Laurel
6. 4500–4799 Cliff
7. Ceres
8. 3400–3899 Mall

9. Delhi
10. Dexter
11. 1900–2299 Laurel
12. 3300–3999 Cliff
13. Cicero
14. 4000–4299 Cliff
15. 2100–2799 Mall
16. Foster

17. Magnet
18. Ceres
19. 2800–3399 Mall
20. 3200–3799 Laurel
21. 4300–4499 Cliff
22. Pearl
23. 3900–4399 Mall
24. Natoma

25. 4800–4999 Cliff
26. 1500–1899 Laurel
27. Cedar
28. 4400–4599 Mall
29. 4500–4799 Cliff
30. Dexter
31. 3000–3199 Laurel
32. Niles

33. Delhi
34. 3900–4399 Mall
35. Cicero
36. Dexter
37. 4800–4999 Cliff
38. 2300–2999 Laurel
39. 2100–2799 Mall
40. 3300–3999 Cliff

41. 3400–3899 Mall
42. 4300–4499 Cliff
43. Ceres
44. Foster
45. Magnet
46. 3200–3799 Laurel
47. Pearl
48. 1500–1899 Laurel

49. 4500–4799 Cliff
50. 1900–2299 Laurel
51. Niles
52. 3300–3999 Cliff
53. 2800–3399 Mall
54. Cicero
55. Delhi
56. 4000–4299 Cliff

57. Dexter
58. Magnet
59. 3000–3199 Laurel
60. 3900–4399 Mall
61. Natoma
62. 3000–3199 Laurel
63. 4300–4499 Cliff
64. Cedar

65. 4400–4599 Mall
66. 1500–1899 Laurel
67. 4800–4999 Cliff
68. Delhi
69. Pearl
70. 2300–2999 Laurel
71. 4500–4799 Cliff
72. Niles

73. 4000–4299 Cliff
74. 3400–3899 Mall
75. 1900–2299 Laurel
76. 2800–3399 Mall
77. Ceres
78. Magnet
79. Cicero
80. 3200–3799 Laurel

81. 3000–3199 Laurel
82. 3900–4399 Mall
83. Natoma
84. 3300–3999 Cliff
85. 3400–3899 Mall
86. Foster
87. 2100–2799 Mall
88. 4300–4499 Cliff

STOP.

If you finish before the time is up, go back and rework the questions on this page only.

SAMPLE ANSWER SHEET

TEST -- LIST 2
KEY (CORRECT ANSWERS)

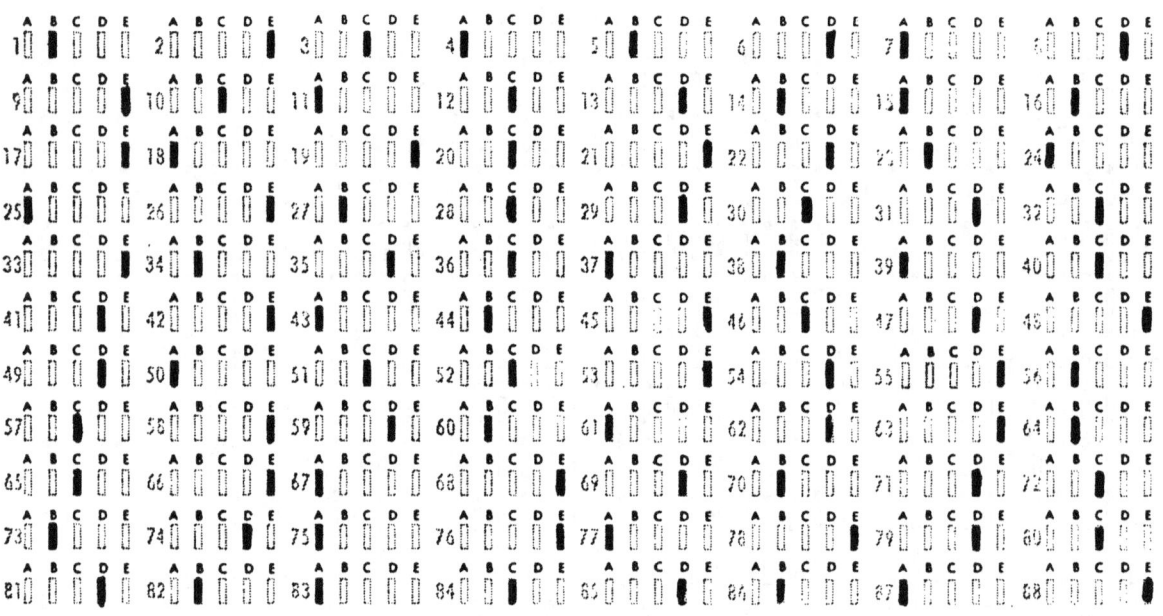

WORD MEANING

SAMPLE QUESTIONS

In both the Clerk-Carrier and Mail Handler examinations, you will have questions about the meaning of words, or vocabulary. There is a word-meaning part in the Mail Handler examination and a word-meaning section in the Clerk-Carrier examination. The words used in the test for Mail Handler are easier than the ones for Clerk-Carrier.

In this kind of question you have to say what a word or phrase means. (A phrase is a group of words.) This word or phrase is in *italics* in a sentence. You are also given for each question five other words or groups of words---lettered A, B, C, D, and E----as possible answers. One of these words or groups of words means the same as the word or group of words in italics. Only one is right. You are to pick out the one that is right and darken the box that has the letter of your answer.

Hints for Answering Word-Meaning Questions
- Read each question carefully.
- Choose the best answer of the five choices even though it is not the word you might use yourself
- Answer first those that you know. Then do the others.
- If you know that some of the suggested answers are not right, pay no more attention to them.
- Be sure that you have marked an answer for every question, even if you have to guess.

Now study the sample questions and explanations before going on to the Practice Tests.
Word Meaning-Sample Questions
Now try a few.

The letter was *short*. *Short* means most nearly
- A. tall
- B. wide
- C. brief
- D. heavy
- E. dark

Short is a word you have used to describe something that is small, or not long, or little, etc. There fore you would not have to spend much time figuring out the right answer. You would choose c) brief

Try another.

The young man is *vigorous*. *Vigorous* means most nearly
- A. serious
- B. reliable
- C. courageous
- D. strong
- E. talented

Vigorous is a word that you have probably used yourself or read somewhere. It carries with it the idea of being active, full of pep, etc. Which one of the five choices comes closest to meaning that? Certainly not A) serious, B) reliable or E) talented; C) courageous-maybe, D) strong-maybe. But between courageous or strong, you would have to agree that strong is the better choice. Therefore you would choose D.

TEST 1

Now that you know what to do, try these. These words are like those in the Mail Handler examination.

For each question, darken the box for the correct answer. Mark your answers on the answer sheet on the next page.

Answer first those questions for which you know the answers. Then work on the other questions. If you can't figure out the answer, guess.

Do not spend more than 30 minutes on this practice test.

1. *Simple* clothing should be worn to work. *Simple* means most nearly

   A. plain
   B. inexpensive
   C. nice
   D. comfortable
   E. old

2. Take your *finished* work to that area of the work floor. *Finished* means most nearly

   A. inspected
   B. assigned
   C. outgoing
   D. completed
   E. rejected

3. If we are not careful, the problem will *develop* further. *Develop* means most nearly

   A. continue
   B. appear
   C. be used
   D. grow
   E. be concerned

4. The mail handler was a *rapid* worker. *Rapid* means most nearly

   A. trained
   B. rash
   C. fast
   D. regular
   E. strong

5. The supply of envelopes is *abundant* for our use. *Abundant* means most nearly

   A. accessible
   B. plentiful
   C. concentrated
   D. divided
   E. scattered

6. The department is working on *experiments* in that area. *Experiments* means most nearly

   A. tests
   B. refinements
   C. statements
   D. plans
   E. patents

7. The members were concerned about two *fundamental* points. *Fundamental* means most nearly

   A. difficult
   B. serious
   C. emphasized
   D. essential
   E. final

8. The leader *asserted* that it was time to start. *Asserted* means most nearly

   A. believed
   B. decided
   C. declared
   D. agreed
   E. contradicted

9. All requests for supplies should be stated *exactly*. *Exactly* means most nearly

   A. briefly
   B. clearly
   C. promptly
   D. emphatically
   E. accurately

10. We had not meant to *alarm* them. *Alarm* means most nearly

    A. endanger
    B. insult
    C. accuse
    D. frighten
    E. confuse

11. The kind of car he bought was *costly*. *Costly* means most nearly

    A. custom made
    B. expensive
    C. desirable
    D. cheap
    E. scarce

12. The cause of the action was *revealed* before the meeting. *Revealed* means most nearly

    A. made known
    B. fully described
    C. carefully hidden
    D. guessed at
    E. seriously questioned

13. The material used to make mail sacks is *durable*. *Durable* means most nearly

    A. thick
    B. waterproof
    C. lasting
    D. elastic
    E. light

14. The *valiant* men and women were rewarded. *Valiant* means most nearly

    A. brave
    B. popular
    C. victorious
    D. loyal
    E. famous

15. The worker was affected by his *fatigue*. *Fatigue* means most nearly

    A. problem
    B. weariness
    C. relaxation
    D. u) sickness
    E. worry

16. The meeting was interrupted by an *urgent* call. *Urgent* means most nearly

    A. trivial
    B. annoying
    C. pressing
    D. surprising
    E. casual

17. The captain of the team will *participate in* the ceremony. *Participate in* means most nearly

    A. depend upon
    B. be recognized at
    C. be invited to
    D. supervise
    E. share in

18. Each office was asked to *restrict* the number of forms it used. *Restrict* means most nearly

    A. watch
    B. record
    C. limit
    D. replace
    E. provide

19. The pole was *rigid*. *Rigid* means most nearly

    A. broken
    B. pointed
    C. bent
    D. rough
    E. stiff

20. The supervisor *demonstrated* the sorting procedure. *Demonstrated* means most nearly

    A. changed
    B. controlled
    C. determined
    D. showed
    E. described

21. The effort was *futile*. *Futile* means most nearly

    A. wasteful
    B. useless
    C. foolish
    D. undesirable
    E. unfortunate

22. There was a pile of *sundry* items on the table. *Sundry* means most nearly

    A. miscellaneous
    B. valuable
    C. unusual
    D. necessary
    E. specific

23. The supervisor should not be *partial*. *Partial* means most nearly

    A. biased
    B. greedy
    C. irresponsible
    D. jealous
    E. suspicious

24. The retired postal worker led an *inactive* life. *Inactive* means most nearly

    A. restful
    B. idle
    C. peaceful
    D. ordinary
    E. weary

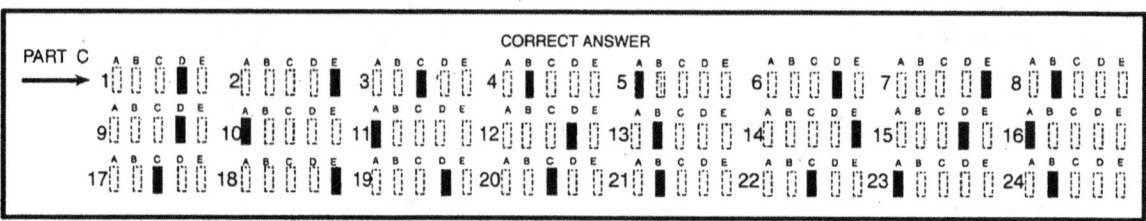

Now check your answers by comparing them with the correct answers shown below.

Count, how many you got right, and write that number on this line _____ _____
(This is your Test Score.)

Meaning of Test Score

If your Test Score is *18 or over,* you have a Good score.
If your Test Score is from *15 to 17, you* have a Fair score.
If your Test Score is *14 or less,* you are not doing too well.

TEST 2

This practice test is a little harder.

For each question, darken the box for the correct answer. Mark your answers on the answer sheet on the next page.

Answer first those questions for which you know the answers. Then work on the other questions. If you can't figure out the answer, guess.

Do not spend more than *30 minutes* on this practice test.

1. The officials *prevented* the action. *Prevented* means most nearly

   A. allowed
   B. urged
   C. hindered
   D. considered
   E. suggested

2. The postmaster's office expected to *report* the results next week. *Report* means most nearly

   A. decide
   B. tell
   C. approve
   D. study
   E. repeat

3. The conference room is now *vacant*. *Vacant* means most nearly

   A. empty
   B. quiet
   C. dark
   D. available
   E. lonely

4. Tapping on the desk can be an *irritating* habit. *Irritating* means most nearly

   A. nervous
   B. annoying
   C. noisy
   D. startling
   E. unsuitable

5. The package was *forwarded* by our office. *Forwarded* means most nearly

   A. returned
   B. canceled
   C. received
   D. detained
   E. sent

6. The postal service is *essential* in this country. *Essential* means most nearly

   A. inevitable
   B. needless
   C. economical
   D. indispensable
   E. established

7. The wheel turned at a *uniform* rate. *Uniform* means most nearly

   A. increasing
   B. unusual
   C. normal
   D. slow
   E. unchanging

8. Each carrier realized his *obligation*. *Obligation* means most nearly

   A. importance
   B. need
   C. duty
   D. n) kindness
   E. honor

9. The group was interested in the *origin* of the rumor. *Origin* means most nearly

   A. direction
   B. growth
   C. existence
   D. beginning
   E. end

10. Laws governing the *parole* of prisoners should be more flexible. *Parole* means most nearly

    A. conditional release
    B. withdrawal of privileges
    C. good behavior
    D. outside employment
    E. solitary confinement

11. That employee is *retiring* by nature. *Retiring* means most nearly

    A. complaining
    B. gruff
    C. neglected
    D. modest
    E. sluggish

12. The patron verified the contents of the package. *Verified* means most nearly

    A. justified
    B. explained
    C. confirmed
    D. guaranteed
    E. examined

13. The group was *repulsed* immediately. *Repulsed* means most nearly

    A. rebuffed
    B. excused
    C. mistreated
    D. loathed
    E. resented

14. The time was right for the committee to make a *decisive* statement. *Decisive* means most nearly

    A. official
    B. prompt
    C. judicial
    D. rational
    E. conclusive

15. Each person expects *compensation* for his work. *Compensation* means most nearly

    A. fulfillment
    B. remuneration
    C. appreciation
    D. approval
    E. recommendation

16. The department plans to increase the number of *novices* in the program. *Novices* means most nearly

    A. volunteers
    B. experts
    C. trainers
    D. beginners
    E. amateurs

17. The guests were overwhelmed by *the fabulous* decorations. *Fabulous* means most nearly

    A. antiquated
    B. enormous
    C. incredible
    D. immoderate
    E. intricate

18. The duties of the job are mentioned *explicitly* in the handbook. *Explicitly* means most nearly

    A. casually
    B. informally
    C. intelligibly
    D. exclusively
    E. specifically

19. The school is supplying opportunities for *recreation*. *Recreation* means most nearly

    A. diversion
    B. eating
    C. resting
    D. learning
    E. recess

20. It was necessary to *recapitulate* the regulation. *Recapitulate* means most nearly

    A. emphasize
    B. withdraw
    C. reinstate
    D. interpret
    E. summarize

21. The villagers *succumbed to* the enemy forces. *Succumbed to* means most nearly

    A. aided
    B. opposed
    C. yielded to
    D. were checked by
    E. discouraged

22. The shipments have been *accelerated*. *Accelerated* means most nearly

    A. anxiously awaited
    B. caused to move faster
    C. delayed by traffic congestion
    D. given careful handling
    E. routed over shorter lines

23. He was not a good employee, because he was *indolent*. *Indolent* means most nearly

    A. stupid
    B. indifferent
    C. selfish
    D. lazy
    E. incompetent

24. He had been cautioned not to be *vindictive*. *Vindictive* means most nearly

    A. boastful
    B. impolite
    C. impulsive
    D. revengeful
    E. aggressive

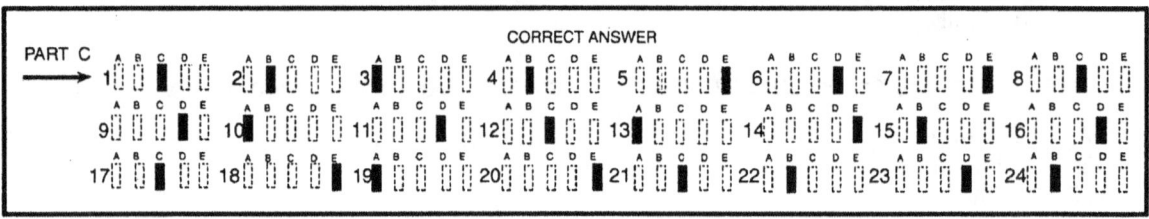

Now check your answers by comparing them with the correct answers shown below.

Count how many you got right, and write that number on this line _____ _____
(This is your Test Score. The meaning of your Test Score will be found on page 3.)

TEST 3

Here is another practice test.

For each question, darken the box for the correct answer. Mark your answers on the answer sheet on the next page.

Answer first those questions for which yon know the answers. Then work on the other questions. If you can't figure out the answer, guess.

Do not spend more than *30 minutes* on this practice test.

1. The *power* of that organization cannot be ignored any longer. *Power* means most nearly

    A. size
    B. courage
    C. success
    D. force
    E. ambition

2. The employees reached the *shore* several days later. *Shore* means most nearly

    A. ocean
    B. reef
    C. island
    D. water
    E. coast

3. The *instructor* was enthusiastic. *Instructor* means most nearly

    A. expert
    B. foreman
    C. teacher
    D. beginner
    E. assistant

4. A *responsible* employee is an asset to any business. *Responsible* means most nearly

    A. considerate
    B. trustworthy
    C. smart
    D. experienced
    E. resourceful

5. He was a good clerk because he was *alert*. *Alert* means most nearly

    A. watchful
    B. busy
    C. honest
    D. helpful
    E. faithful

6. The machine was *revolving* rapidly. *Revolving* means most nearly

    A. working
    B. inclining
    C. vibrating
    D. n) turning
    E. producing

7. The canceling machine did not *function* yesterday. *Function* means most nearly

    A. finish
    B. stop
    C. overheat
    D. vibrate
    E. operate

127

8. The supervisor did not *comprehend* the clerk's excuse. *Comprehend* means most nearly

   A. hear
   B. understand
   C. suspect
   D. consider
   E. accept

9. His conduct was *becoming*. *Becoming* means most nearly

   A. improved
   B. heroic
   C. deliberate
   D. suitable
   E. patient

10. The men were not aware of the *hazard*. *Hazard* means most nearly

    A. peril
    B. choice
    C. decision
    D. contest
    E. damage

11. A *flexible* policy was developed to handle the situation. *Flexible* means most nearly

    A. pliable
    B. weak
    C. rigid
    D. uniform
    E. active

12. The clerk suggested an *innovation*. *Innovation* means most nearly

    A. conventional practice
    B. improvement
    C. inadequate change
    D. new method
    E. preliminary trial

    12.___

13. Many parents *indulge* their children too much. *Indulge* means most nearly

    A. admire
    B. humor
    C. flatter
    D. coax
    E. discipline

14. The men were *commended* for their actions during the emergency. *Commended* means most nearly

    A. blamed
    B. reprimanded
    C. promoted
    D. encouraged
    E. praised

15. Two men were *designated* by the postmaster. *Designated* means most nearly

    A. dismissed
    B. assisted
    C. instructed
    D. named
    E. rebuked

16. The package will be *conveyed* by the employees. *Conveyed* means most nearly

    A. carried
    B. wrapped
    C. exchanged
    D. refused
    E. guarded

17. It seems *feasible* to start the physical fitness training now. *Feasible* means most nearly

    A. praiseworthy
    B. justifiable
    C. practicable
    D. beneficial
    E. profitable

18. He was a *notorious* rebel. *Notorious* means most nearly

    A. condemned
    B. unpleasant
    C. vexatious
    D. pretentious
    E. well-known

19. The main speaker appeared to be a *pompous* person. *Pompous* means most nearly

    A. narrow-minded
    B. insincere
    C. talkative
    D. self-important
    E. rude

20. The office was surprised that he had *disregarded* his duty. *Disregarded* means most nearly

    A. contemplated
    B. discerned
    C. neglected
    D. resisted
    E. renounced

21. The collector described the *blemish* on the new stamp. *Blemish* means most nearly

    A. color
    B. flaw
    C. design
    D. imprint
    E. figure

22. The *ardor* of the patriot was contagious. *Ardor* means most nearly

    A. anger
    B. desire
    C. zeal
    D. happiness
    E. daring

23. All the employees *vied* for that award. *Vied* means most nearly

    A. contended
    B. cooperated
    C. petitioned
    D. persevered
    E. prepared

24. Immediately after hearing the bad news, the group was in a state of *ferment*. *Ferment* means most nearly

    A. lawlessness
    B. indecision
    C. disintegration
    D. reorganization
    E. agitation

4 (#3)

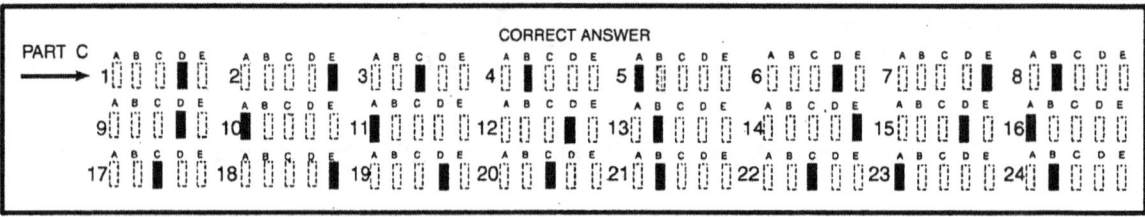

Now check your answers by comparing them with the correct answers shown below.

Count how many you got right, and write that number on this line _____ _____
(This is your Test Score. The meaning of your Test Score will be found on page 3.)

READING COMPREHENSION

DESCRIPTION OF THE TEST AND SAMPLE QUESTIONS

On the job both Clerks and Carriers have to read and understand Post Office publications. This test measures how well you understand what you read. This is how it is done: You read a short paragraph and five statements. From the five statements, you choose the one statement, or answer, that is best supported by, or best matches, what is said in the paragraph.

Try one:

"The prevention of accidents makes it necessary not only that safety devices be used to guard exposed machinery but also that mechanics be instructed in safety rules which they must follow for their own protection and that the light in the plant be adequate."
The paragraph BEST supports the statement that industrial accidents
- A. are always avoidable
- B. may be due to ignorance
- C. usually result from inadequate machinery
- D. cannot be entirely overcome
- E. result in damage to machinery

Remember what you have to do:
First: Read the paragraph
Second: Decide what the paragraph means
Third: Read the five suggested answers
Fourth: Select the one answer which best matches what the paragraph says or is best supported by something in the paragraph. (Sometimes you may have to read the paragraph again in order to be sure which suggested answer is best.)

This paragraph is talking about three steps that should be taken to prevent industrial accidents:
1. Use safety devices on machines
2. Instruct mechanics in safety rules
3. Provide adequate lighting

With this in mind, let's look at each suggested answer. Each one starts with "Industrial accidents."

So the first one reads: Industrial accidents (A) are always avoidable. (The paragraph talks about how to avoid accidents, but does not say that accidents are *always* avoidable.)

Second: Industrial accidents (B) may be due to ignorance. (One of the steps given in the paragraph to prevent accidents is to instruct mechanics on safety rules. This suggests that lack of knowledge or ignorance of safety rules causes accidents. This suggested answer sounds like a good possibility for being the right answer.)

Third: Industrial accidents (C) usually result from inadequate machinery. (The paragraph does suggest that exposed machines cause accidents, but it doesn't say that it is the usual cause of accidents. The word *usually* makes this a wrong answer.)

Fourth: Industrial accidents (D) cannot be entirely overcome. (You may know from your own experience that this is a true statement. But that is not what the paragraph is talking about. Therefore, it is not the correct answer.)

Fifth: Industrial accidents (E) result in damage to machinery. (This is a statement that may or may not be true, but in any case it is not covered by the paragraph.)

Looking back, you see that the one suggested answers of the five given that BEST matches *what the paragraph says* is: Industrial accidents (B) may be due to ignorance.

Be sure you read *all* the possible answers before you make your choice. You may think that none of the five answers is really good, but choose the best one of the five.

Here is another:

"Probably few people realize, as they drive on a concrete road, that steel is used to keep the surface flat in spite of the weight of buses and trucks. Steel bars deeply embedded in the concrete provide sinews to take the stress so that the stress cannot crack the slab or make it wavy."

Now read and think about the possible answers:
- A. A concrete road is expensive to build.
  (Maybe so but that is not what the paragraph is about.)

- B. A concrete road usually cracks under heavy weights.
  (The paragraph talks about using steel bars to prevent heavy weights from cracking concrete roads. It says nothing about how usual it is for the roads to crack. The word *usually* makes this suggested answer wrong.)

- C. A concrete road looks like any other road.
  (This may or may not be true. The important thing to note is that it has nothing to do with what the paragraph is about.)

- D. A concrete road is used only for heavy traffic.
  (This answer at least has something to do with the paragraph—concrete roads are used with heavy traffic but it does not say "used only.")

- E. A concrete road is reinforced with other material.
  (This choice seems to be the correct one on two counts. First, the paragraph does suggest that concrete roads are made stronger by embedding steel bars in them. This is another way of saying "concrete roads are reinforced with steel bars." Second, by the process of elimination, the other four choices are ruled out as correct answers simply because they do not apply.)

You can be sure that not all the reading questions will be as easy as these.

Hints for Answering Reading Questions
- Read the paragraph carefully. Then read each suggested answer carefully. Read every word, because often one word can make the difference between a right and a wrong answer.

- Choose that answer which is supported in the paragraph itself. Do not choose an answer which is a correct statement unless it is based on information in the paragraph.
- Even though a suggested answer has many of the words used in the paragraph, it may still be wrong.
- Look out for words—such as always, never, entirely, or only—which end to make a suggested answer wrong.
- Answer first those questions which you can answer most easily. Then work on the other questions.

If you can't figure out the answer to a question, guess.

Reading—Sample Questions

Here are some sample questions for you to try. Remember to read the paragraph carefully. Then select the answer (A, B, C, D, or E) which is best supported by the paragraph.

Mark your answers for the sample questions in the space at the right.

1. "Post Office clerks assigned to stamp-windows are directly responsible financially in the selling of postage. In addition, they are expected to have a thorough knowledge as to the acceptability of matter offered for mailing. Any information which they give out to the public must be accurate."
   The paragraph BEST supports the statement that *clerks assigned to stamp-window duty*
   A. must account for stamps issued to them for sale
   B. have had long training in other post-office work
   C. advise the public only on matters of official business
   D. must refer continuously to the sources of postal regulations
   E. inspect the contents of every package offered for mailing

   1.____

   Did you pick out in your mind the important points made in the paragraph?
   Did you read over all the answers before picking one?
   Did you rule out the ones you know are wrong?
   Did you pick A?

Here is another:

2. "The leader of an industrial enterprise has two principal functions. He must manufacture and distribute a product at a profit and he must keep individuals and groups of individuals working effectively together."
   The paragraph BEST supports the statement that *an industrial leader should be able to*
   A. increase the distribution of his plant's products
   B. introduce large-scale production methods
   C. coordinate the activities of employees
   D. profit by the experienced of other leaders
   E. expand the business rapidly

   2.____

Don't be fooled by answers which you may know are true statements but are not covered by the paragraph.

3. "Numerous benefits to the employer as well as to the worker have resulted from physical examinations of employees. Such examinations are intended primarily as a means of increasing efficiency and production, and they have been found to accomplish these ends."
The paragraph BEST supports the statement that *physical examinations*
   A. may serve to increase output
   B. are a source of greater gain to employers than to employees
   C. are required in some plants
   D. often reveal serious defects previously unknown
   E. always are worth more than they cost

4. "The traffic congestion in many American cities is chiefly due to the fact that the increase in the floor area of buildings has been greater than the improvement in methods of handling traffic."
The paragraph BEST supports the statement that *in many cities*
   A. buildings are erected at the points where most people gather
   B. little improvement has been made in handling traffic
   C. the floor area of the buildings should not be greater than the street areas
   D. the provision for traffic has not kept pace with the increase in floor areas
   E. traffic rules are difficult to enforce in busy sections

5. "The telegraph networks of the country now constitute wonderfully operated institutions, affording for ordinary use of modern business an important means of communication. The transmission of messages by electricity has reached the goal for which the postal service has long been striving, namely, the elimination of distance as an effective barrier of communication."
The quotation BEST supports the statement that
   A. a new standard of communication has been attained
   B. in the telegraph service, messages seldom go astray
   C. it is the distance between the parties which creates the need for communication
   D. modern business relies more upon the telegraph than upon the mails
   E. the telegraph is a form of postal service

KEY (CORRECT ANSWERS)

1. A
2. C
3. A
4. D
5. A

READING—PRACTICE TEST 1

DIRECTIONS: For each question, read the paragraph and then select the suggested answer that is BEST supported by the paragraph. *PRINT THE LETTER OF THE CORRECT ANSWER IN THE SPACE AT THE RIGHT.*

1. "Any business not provided with capable substitutes to fill all important positions is a weak business. Therefore, a foreman should train each man not only to perform his own particular duties, but also to do those of two or three positions."
   The paragraph BEST supports the statement that
   A. dependence on substitutes is a sign of a weak organization
   B. training will improve the strongest organization
   C. the foreman should be the most expert at any particular job under him
   D. every employee can be trained to perform efficiently work other than his own
   E. vacancies in vital positions should be provided for in advance

2. "The coloration of textile fabrics composed of cotton and wool generally requires two processes, as the process used in dyeing wool is seldom capable of fixing the color upon cotton. The usual method is to immerse the fabric in the requisite baths to dye the wool and then to treat the partially dyed material in the manner found suitable for cotton."
   The paragraph BEST supports the statement that that the dyeing of textile fabrics composed of cotton and wool
   A. is less complicated than the dyeing of wool alone
   B. is more successful when the material contains more cotton than wool
   C. is not satisfactory when solid colors are desired
   D. is restricted to two colors for any one fabric
   E. is usually based upon the methods required for dyeing the different materials

3. "The Federal investigator must direct his whole effort toward success in his work. If he wishes to succeed in each investigation, his work will be by no means easy, smooth, or peaceful; on the contrary, he will have to devote himself completely and continuously to a task that requires all his ability."
   The paragraph BEST supports the statement that an investigator's success depends most upon
   A. ambition to advance rapidly in the service
   B. persistence in the face of difficulty
   C. training and experience
   D. willingness to obey orders without delay
   E. the number of investigations which he conducts

4. "Honest people in one nation find it difficult to understand the viewpoint of honest people in another. State departments and their ministers exist for the purpose of explaining the viewpoints of one nation in terms understood by another. Some of their most important work lies in this direction."
   The paragraph BEST supports the statement that
   A. people of different nations may not consider matters in the same light
   B. it is unusual for many people to share similar ideas
   C. suspicion prevents understanding between nations
   D. the chief work of state departments is to guide relations between nations united by a common cause
   E. the people of one nation must sympathize with the viewpoints of others

4.____

5. "Economy once in a while is just not enough. I expect to find it at every level of responsibility, from cabinet member to the newest and youngest recruit. Controlling waste is something like bailing a boat; you have to keep at it. I have no intention of easing up on my insistence on getting a dollar of value for each dollar we spend."
   The paragraph BEST supports the statement that
   A. we need not be concerned about items which cost less than a dollar
   B. it is advisable to buy the cheaper of two items
   C. the responsibility of economy is greater at high levels than at low levels
   D. economy becomes easy with practice
   E. economy is a continuing responsibility

5.____

6. "On all permit imprint mail the charge for postage has been printed by the mailer before he presents it for mailing and pays the postage. Such mail of any class is mailable only at the post office that issued a permit covering it. Since the postage receipts for such mail represent only the amount of permit imprint mail detected and verified, employees in receiving, handling, and outgoing sections must be alert constantly to route such mail to the weighing section before it is handled or dispatched."
   The paragraph BEST supports the statement that, at post offices where permit mail is received for dispatch,
   A. dispatching units make a final check on the amount of postage payable on permit imprint mail
   B. employees are to check the postage chargeable on mail received under permit
   C. neither more nor less postage is to be collected than the amount printed on permit imprint mail
   D. the weighing section is primarily responsible for failure to collect postage on such mail
   E. unusual measures are taken to prevent unstamped mail from being accepted.

6.____

7. "Education should not stop when the individual has been prepared to make a livelihood and to live in modern society. Living would be mere existence were there no appreciation and enjoyment of the riches of art, literature, and science.

7.____

The paragraph BEST supports the statement that true education
- A. is focused on the routine problems of life
- B. prepares one for full enjoyment of life
- C. deals chiefly with art, literature, and science
- D. is not possible for one who does not enjoy scientific literature
- E. disregards practical ends

8. "Insured and c.o.d. air and surface mail is accepted with the understanding that the sender guarantees any necessary forwarding or return postage. When such mail is forwarded or returned, it shall be rated up for collection of postage; except that insured or c.o.d. air mail weighing 8 ounces or less and subject to the 10 cents an ounce rate shall be forwarded b air if delivery will be advanced, and returned by surface means, without additional postage."
The paragraph BEST supports the statement that the return postage for undeliverable insured mail is
- A. included in the original prepayment on air mail parcels
- B. computed but not collected before dispatching surface parcel post mail to sender
- C. not computed or charged for any air mail that is returned by surface transportation
- D. included in the amount collected when the sender mails parcel post
- E. collected before dispatching for return if any amount due has been guaranteed

8.____

9. "All undeliverable first-class mail, except first-class parcels and parcel-post paid with first-class postage, which cannot be returned to the sender, is sent to a dead-letter branch. Undeliverable matter of the third- and fourth-classes of obvious value for which the sender does not furnish return postage and undeliverable first-class parcels and parcel-post matter bearing postage of the first-class, which cannot be returned, is sent to a dead parcel-post branch."
The paragraph BEST supports the statement that matter that is sent to a dead parcel-post branch includes all undeliverable
- A. mail, except first-class letter mail, that appears to be valuable
- B. mail, except that of the first-class, on which the sender failed to prepay the original mailing costs
- C. parcels on which the mailer prepaid the first-class rate of postage
- D. third- and fourth-class matter on which the required return postage has not been paid
- E. parcels on which first-class postage has been prepaid, when the sender's address is not known

9.____

10. "Civilization started to move rapidly when man freed himself of the shackles that restricted his search for truth.
The paragraph BEST supports the statement that the progress of civilization
- A. came as a result of man's dislike for obstacles
- B. did not begin until restrictions on learning were removed
- C. has been aided by man's efforts to find the truth
- D. is based on continually increasing efforts
- E. continues at a constantly increasing rate

10.____

KEY (CORRECT ANSWERS)

1.	E	6.	B
2.	E	7.	B
3.	B	8.	B
4.	A	9.	E
5.	E	10.	C

READING—PRACTICE TEST 2

DIRECTIONS: For each question, read the paragraph and then select the suggested answer that is BEST supported by the paragraph. *PRINT THE LETTER OF THE CORRECT ANSWER IN THE SPACE AT THE RIGHT.*

1. "A city directory, where available, interleaved with suitable blank leaves and subdivided into a number of volumes equal to the maximum number of employees assigned to directory work at one time, shall be used to give directory service. Where a city directory is not published, a telephone directory, if available, may be used. Dual use of a city directory and a telephone directory shall be confined to firm, insured, c.o.d., special handling, and special delivery mail."
   The paragraph BEST supports the statement that the use of a city directory
   A. at times may be supplemented by the use of a telephone directory
   B. is of little value unless postal directory service is kept current
   C. is less productive than is the use of a telephone directory
   D. is to be confined to insured, c.o.d., and special delivery mail
   E. provides more accurate information than does the use of a telephone directory

   1.____

2. "Taxes are deducted each pay period from the amount of salaries or wages, including payments for overtime and night differential, paid to employees of the postal service in excess of the withholding exemptions allowed under the Internal Revenue Act. The amount of tax to be withheld from each payment of wages to any employee, except fourth-class postmasters, will be determined from the current official table of pay and withholding exemptions published by the Post Office Department."
   The paragraph BEST supports the statement that the salaries of most postal employees
   A. are paid in amounts depending upon the exemptions fixed by the Department
   B. do not include overtime or night differential payments
   C. are determined by provisions of the Internal Revenue Act
   D. include taxable overtime or night differential payments that are due each pay period
   E. are subject to tax deductions if the salaries are greater than exemptions

   2.____

3. "Telegrams should be clear, concise, and brief. Omit all unnecessary words. The parts of speech most often used in telegrams are nouns, verbs, adjectives, and adverbs. If possible, do without pronouns, prepositions, articles, and copulative verbs. Use simple sentences, rather than complex and compound."
   The paragraph BEST supports the statement that in writing telegrams one should always use
   A. common and simple words
   B. only nouns, verbs, adjectives, and adverbs
   C. incomplete sentences
   D. only words essential to the meaning
   E. the present tense of verbs

   3.____

4. "The Suggestion System is conducted to give thorough and understanding study to ideas presented by postal employees for promoting the welfare of postal personnel and for improving mail handling and other postal business; and to encourage and reward postal employees who think out, develop, and present acceptable ideas and plans. Through this system, the talent and ability of postal employees are to be used for improving postal service and reducing expenses."
The paragraph BEST supports the statement that one purpose of the Suggestion System is to
   A. maintain a unit of experienced employees to plan and develop improvements
   B. obtain ideas that will help postal employees improve their work
   C. offer promotions to postal employees who suggest useful changes in service
   D. provide pay raises for employees who increase their output
   E. reduce postal operating expense by limiting postal service

4.____

5. "Metered mail must bear the correct date of mailing in the meter impression. When metered mail bearing the wrong date or time is presented for mailing, it shall be run through the canceling machine or otherwise postmarked to show the proper date and time, and then dispatched. The irregularity shall be called to the attention of the mailer. If the irregularity is repeated, the mail may be refused."
The paragraph BEST supports the statement that, if a first mailing of metered mail bears a wrong date or time,
   A. no action shall be taken by the postal service
   B. the mailing privileges of the sender may be canceled
   C. the mailer will not be permitted to submit additional improperly prepared mail
   D. the mailer will be notified of the error before the mail is dispatched
   E. the postal service accepts the responsibility for correction

5.____

6. "Through advertising, manufacturers exercise a high degree of control over consumers' desires. However, the manufacturer assumes enormous risks in attempting to predict what consumers will want and in producing goods in quantity and distributing them in advance of final selection by the consumers."
The paragraph BEST supports the statement that manufacturers
   A. can eliminate the risk of overproduction by advertising
   B. completely control buyers' needs and desires
   C. must depend upon the final consumers for the success of their undertakings
   D. distribute goods directly to the consumers
   E. can predict with great accuracy the success of any product they put on the market

6.____

7. "In the business districts of cities, collections from street letter boxes are made at stated hours, and collectors are required to observe these hours exactly. Any businessman using these boxes can rely with certainty upon the time of the next collection."

7.____

The paragraph BEST supports the statement that mail
- A. collections are both efficient and inexpensive
- B. collections in business districts are more frequent during the day than at night
- C. collectors are required to observe safety regulations exactly
- D. collections are made often in business districts
- E. is collected in business districts on a regular schedule

8. "The function of business is to increase the wealth of the country and the value and happiness of life. It does this by supplying the material needs of men and women. When the nation's business is successfully carried on, it renders public service of the highest value."
The paragraph BEST supports the statement that
- A. all businesses which render public service are successful
- B. human happiness is enhanced only by the increase of material wants
- C. the value of life is increased only by the increase of wealth
- D. the material needs of men and women are supplied by well-conducted business
- E. business is the only field of activity which increases happiness

8.____

9. "In almost every community, fortunately, there are certain men and women known to be public-spirited. Others, however, may be selfish and act only as their private interests seem to require."
The paragraph BEST supports the statement that
- A. fortunate
- B. needed
- C. found only in small communities
- D. not known
- E. not public-spirited

9.____

10. "Whenever two groups of people whose interests at the moment conflict meet to discuss a solution of that conflict, there is laid a basis for an interchange of facts and ideas which increases the total range of knowledge of both parties and tends to break down the barrier which their restricted field of information has helped to create."
The paragraph BEST supports the statement that conflicts between two parties may be brought closer to a settlement through
- A. frank acknowledgment of error
- B. the exchange of accusations
- C. gaining a wider knowledge of facts
- D. submitting the dispute to an impartial judge
- E. limiting discussion to plans acceptable to both groups

10.____

KEY (CORRECT ANSWERS)

1.	A	6.	C
2.	E	7.	E
3.	D	8.	D
4.	B	9.	E
5.	E	10.	C

READING—PRACTICE TEST 3

DIRECTIONS: For each question, read the paragraph and then select the suggested answer that is BEST supported by the paragraph. *PRINT THE LETTER OF THE CORRECT ANSWER IN THE SPACE AT THE RIGHT.*

1. "Carriers shall be careful to deliver mail to the persons for whom it is intended or to someone authorized to receive it. In case of doubt, they shall make inquiry to ascertain the owner. Failing in this, they shall return the mail to the post office for disposition."
   The paragraph BEST supports the statement that, if a carrier has an ordinary letter for delivery, he must
   A. ask the neighbors to identify the addressee before delivering the letter
   B. deliver it only to the address placed on the letter by the sender
   C. never return the letter to the post office if he has definite knowledge of an addressee's address
   D. not deliver the letter if more than one unidentified person claims to be the addressee
   E. return it to the post office if the addressee is not at home

   1.____

2. "Letter carriers, whether assigned to delivery or collection duty, and special-delivery messengers shall receive all prepaid matter bearing a special-delivery stamp, or the equivalent thereof, which may be handed to them on their trips or runs, and shall keep such matter separate from other mail, and turn it in immediately upon their arrival at the post office."
   The paragraph BEST supports the statement that a letter carrier on delivery duty shall accept from a patron
   A. mail bearing a special-delivery stamp or unstamped mail and money for the stamp
   B. all prepaid mail handed to him and turn it in promptly at the post office
   C. special-delivery mail fully prepaid by stamps, and deliver it to the post office
   D. mail for which he receives a special-delivery fee, and keep it separate from ordinary mail
   E. special-delivery mail for posting, but make no deliveries of special-delivery mail

   2.____

3. "Formerly it was only unskilled labor which was shifted from place to place in the wake of industrial booms. Since so many business concerns have become nationwide in the fields they cover, the white-collar workers have been in a similar state of flux."
   The paragraph BEST supports the statement that the growth of big business has resulted in
   A. a shifting supply of unskilled labor
   B. an increased tendency toward movement of workers
   C. an increased proportion of white-collar jobs
   D. the stabilization of industrial booms
   E. the use of fewer workers to do equal work

   3.____

4. "Collections are made by all delivery-carriers in connection with their regular delivery trips, except in the larger post offices, where it has been found necessary to maintain a collection service in business sections during delivery hours. Under ordinary conditions, no mounted collection is needed in strictly residential territory during the time delivery carriers are at work."
The paragraph BEST supports the statement that at small post offices that have delivery service, mail collections
   A. are not made on many residential routes by mounted carriers
   B. ordinarily are not made on residential routes during delivery periods
   C. are made in all business and residential districts by carriers on delivery routes
   D. usually are made by mounted collectors when the amount of mail is large
   E. are made only by delivery carriers in business districts

4.____

5. "In accordance with the ancient principle that a sovereign state may not be sued without its consent, a special Court of Claims has been established in each of several states of the United States. In this court, claims may be brought against the state. However, the state legislature must make the necessary appropriation before the claim awarded by the court can be paid."
The paragraph BEST supports the statement that a
   A. sovereign state cannot be sued by its citizens
   B. claim against a state can only be brought with the approval of the state legislature
   C. sovereign state can only be sued by a Court of Claims
   D. Court of Claims does not have the authority to enforce payment of approved claims
   E. resident or business firm of any state has the right to bring suit against that state

5.____

6. "What constitutes skill in any line of work is not always easy to determine; economy of time must be carefully distinguished from economy of energy, as the quickest method may require the greatest expenditure of muscular effort, and may not be essential or at all desirable."
The paragraph BEST supports the statement that
   A. the most efficiently executed task is not always the one done in the shortest time
   B. energy and time cannot both be conserved in performing a single task
   C. if a task requires muscular energy it is not being performed economically
   D. skill in performing a task should not be acquired at the expense of time
   E. a task is well done when it is performed in the shortest time

6.____

7. "When a number of letters are deposited in a letter box without stamps affixed and a sum of money is found in the box which is not sufficient to pay one full rate of postage on all of the letters, they shall, if mailed by the same person and if he is known and resides within the delivery limit of the mailing office, be returned to him, together with the money. The letters shall be treated as 'Held for Postage' if the sender is unknown or resides beyond the delivery limit of the mailing office."

7.____

The paragraph BEST supports the statement that, when unstamped letters and money are placed in a mailbox by the sender,
- A. the letters are held for postage if sender is unknown and the money is insufficient to pay one full rate on each letter
- B. the letters for which sufficient postage is paid are dispatched, and the others are held
- C. the letters will be returned if the amount of money is insufficient for full postage and the sender lives in another city
- D. only a full return address on the envelope will insure prompt dispatch of the letters
- E. the postal service is not obliged to dispatch such mail even if the money covers full postage

8. "When a card money order is presented for payment, the paying employee shall examine it to see that it is properly drawn and stamped by the issuing post office, and assure himself that it is not issued on a form reported stolen, and that it is signed and presented by the payee or remitter or by a person authorized by either to receive payment. Payment must not be refused if one year or more has elapsed since the last day of the month in which the order was issued.
The paragraph BEST supports the statement that payment for an otherwise correct card money order will not be refused if the order
   - A. was issued by a post office that has since been discontinued
   - B. bears the stamp of a post office other than the one that issued the order
   - C. bears a date more than a year earlier than the date payment is requested
   - D. is presented for payment by a person whose signature is unfamiliar to the paying clerk
   - E. is signed by a person other than the payee or a person authorized by the remitter

8._____

9. "If a parcel originating in another country proves to be undeliverable in the United States owing to the removal of the addressee to a known address in the country where the parcel was mailed, and if the parcel does not bear the sender's instructions for delivery to a second address or for abandonment, it shall be marked 'Parti (removed)' followed by an indication of the forwarding address of the addressee, and treated for return to the country of origin."
The paragraph BEST supports the statement that if the sender has not authorized other delivery or abandonment of an undeliverable parcel, but addressee's new address in sender's country is known, the
   - A. parcel should be marked and forwarded to the address
   - B. sender's instructions should be followed, by returning the parcel to him
   - C. parcel should be prepared to permit return to and forwarding in the sender's country
   - D. return of the parcel should be planned and accomplished promptly
   - E. postal service in the country of origin should inquire how to dispose of the parcel

9._____

10. "The post office of delivery shall require the addressee, or his authorized representative, to open a bad-order registered article, whether repaired with sealing stamps or re-enclosed, in the presence of the delivering employee, the envelope being cut at the end so as to preserve the sealing intact. If any of the contents is missing, the envelope (letter and penalty, if any) or wrapper shall be obtained from the addressee, with his endorsement as to shortage of contents, and sent to the proper inspector in charge with a report of the facts."

The paragraph BEST supports the statement that a bad-order registered article
   A. should be repaired or re-enclosed and sent with a report to the inspector in charge
   B. must be delivered to the addressee only and opened by him in the presence of the delivering employee
   C. is not likely to be received by the addressee with its contents intact
   D. should be checked as to contents, upon delivery, in the presence of the delivering employee
   E. will not be intact upon delivery if the sealing stamps have been tampered with

KEY (CORRECT ANSWERS)

1.	D	6.	A
2.	C	7.	A
3.	B	8.	C
4.	C	9.	C
5.	D	10.	D

Number Series

DESCRIPTION OF THE TEST AND SAMPLE QUESTIONS

This test measures your ability to think with numbers instead of words.

In each problem, you are given a series of numbers that are changing according to a rulefollowed by five sets of 2 numbers each. Your problem is to figure out a rule that would make one of the five sets the next two numbers in the series.

The problems do not use hard arithmetic. The task is merely to see how the numbers are related to each other. The sample questions will explain several types in detail so that you may become familiar with what you have to do.

Hints for Answering Number Series Questions

- Do the ones that are easiest for you first. Then go back and work on the others. Enough time is allowed for you to do all the questions, providing you don't stay too long on the ones you have trouble answering.
- Sound out the series to yourself. You may hear the rule: 2 4 6 8 10 12 14 ... What are the next two numbers?
- Look at the series carefully. You may see the rule: 9 2 9 4 9 6 9 ... What are the next two numbers?
- If you can't hear it or see it, you may have to figure it out by writing down how the numbers are changing: 6 8 16 18 26 28 36 ... What are the next two numbers?
  6^{+2} 8^{+8} 16^{+2} 18^{+8} 26^{+2} 28^{+8} 36 ... What are the next two numbers if this is +2 +8? 36+2=38+8=46 or 38 46. You would mark the letter of the answer that goes with 38 46.
- If none of the answers given fit the rule you have figured out, try again. Try to figure out a rule that makes one of the five answers a correct one.

DON'T SPEND TOO MUCH TIME ON ANY ONE QUESTION. SKIP IT AND COME BACK. A FRESH LOOK SOMETIMES HELPS.

Number Series - Sample Questions

Let's try a few
Mark your answers for these samples on the Sample Answer Sheet on this page.

1. 1 2 3 4 5 6 7 ....A) 1 2   B) 5 6   c) 8 9   D) 4 5   E) 7 8
How are these numbers changing? The numbers in this series are increasing by 1 or the rule is "add 1." If you apply this rule to the series, what would the next two numbers be? 7+1=8+1=9. Therefore, the correct answer is 8 and 9, and you would select c) 8 9 as your answer.

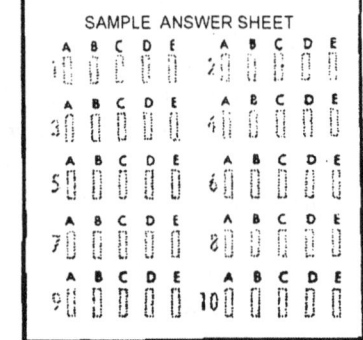

2. 15 14 13 12 11 10 9 .....A) 2 1   B) 17 16   c) 8 9   D) 8 7   E) 9 8
The numbers in this series are decreasing by 1 or the rule is "subtract 1. " If you apply that rule, what would the next two numbers be? 91=81 = 7. The correct answer is 8 and 7, and you would select D) 8 7 as your answer.

3. 20 20 21 21 22 22 23........A) 23 23   B) 23 24   c) 19 19   D) 22 23   E) 21 22
In this series each number is repeated and then increased by 1. The rule is "repeat, add 1, repeat, add 1,
etc." The series would be 20^{+0} 20^{+1} 21^{+0} 21^{+1} 22^{+0} 22^{+1} 23^{+0} 23^{+1} 24. The correct answer is 23 and 24, and you should have darkened B on the Sample Answer Sheet for question 3.

4. 17 3 17 4 17 5 17..........A) 6 17   B) 6 7   c) 17 6   D) 5 6   E) 17 7
If you can't find a single rule for all the numbers in a series, see if there are really two series in the problem. This series is the number 17 separated by numbers increasing by 1, starting with 3. If the series were continued for two more numbers, it would read 17 3 17 4 17 5 17 6 17. The correct answer is 6 and 17, and you should have darkened A on the Sample Answer Sheet for question 4.

5. 1 2 4 5 7 8 10...............A) 11 12   B) 12 14   c) 10 13   D) 12 13   E) 11 13
The rule in this series is not easy to see until you actually set down how the numbers are changing: 1^{+1} 2^{+2} 4^{+1} 5^{+2} 7^{+1} 8^{+2} 10. The numbers in this series are increasing first by 1 (that is plus 1) and then by 2 (that is plus 2). If the series were continued for two more numbers, it would read: 1245 7 8 10 (plus 1) which is 11 (plus 2) which is 13. Therefore the correct answer is 11 and 13, and you should have darkened E on the Sample Answer Sheet for question 5.

Now read and work sample questions 6 through 10 and mark your answers on the Sample Answer Sheet on this page.

6. 21 21 20 20 19 19 18 ....A) 18 18   B) 18 17   C) 17 18   D) 17 17   E) 18 19
7. 1 22 1 23 1 24 1 ....A) 2 61   B) 25 26   C) 25 1   D) 1 26   E) 1 25
8. 1 20 3 19 5 18 7 ....A) 8 9   B) 8 17   C) 17 10   D) 17 9   E) 9 18
9. 4 7 10 13 16 19 22 ....A) 23 26   B) 25 27   C) 25 26   D) 25 28   E) 24 27
10. 30 2 28 4 26 6 24 ....A) 23 9   B) 26 8   C) 8 9   D) 26 22   E) 8 22

The correct answers to sample questions 6 to 10 are: 6B, 7c, 8D, 9D, and 10E.

Explanations for questions 6 through 10.

6. Each number in the series repeats itself and then decreases by 1 or minus 1; *21* (repeat) *21* (minus 1) which makes *20* (repeat) *20* (minus 1) which makes *19* (repeat) *19* (minus 1) which makes *18* (repeat) ? (minus 1) ?

7. The number *1* is separated by numbers which begin with *22* and increase by 1; *1 22 1* (increase 22 by 1) which makes *23 1* (increase 23 by 1) which makes *24 1* (increase 24 by 1) which makes ?

8. This is best explained by two alternating series—one series starts with *1* and increases by 2 or plus 2; the other series starts with *20* and decreases by 1 or minus 1.

    1↑3↑5↑7↑?
    20 19 18 ?

9. This series of numbers increases by 3 (plus 3) beginning with the first number *4* (plus 3) *7* (plus 3) *10* (plus 3) *13* (plus 3) *16* (plus 3) *19*. (plus 3) *22* (plus 3) ? (plus 3) ?

10. Look for two alternating series—one series starts with *30* and decreases by 2 (minus 2); the other series starts with *2* and increases by 2 (plus 2).

    30↑28↑26↑24↑?
    2 4 6 ?

Now try questions 11 to 18. Mark your answers on the Sample Answer Sheet on this page.

11. 5 6 20 7 8 19 9 ....A) 10 18 B) 18 17 C) 10 17 D) 18 19 E) 10 11
12. 9 10 1 11 12 2 13 ....A) 2 14   B) 3 14   C) 14 3   D) 14 15 E) 14 1
13. 4 6 9 11 14 16 19 ....A) 21 24 B) 22 25 C) 20 22 D) 21 23 E) 22 24
14. 8 8 1 10 10 3 12 ....A) 13 13 B) 12 5   C) 12 4   D) 13 5   E) 4 12
15. 14 1 2 15 3 4 16 ....A) 5 16   B) 6 7   C) 5 17   D) 5 6   E) 17 5
16. 10 12 50 15 17 50 20 ....A) 50 21 B) 21 50 C) 50 22 D) 22 50 E) 22 24
17. 1 2 3 50 4 5 6 51 7 8 ....A) 9 10   B) 9 52   C) 51 10 D) 10 52 E) 10 50
18. 20 21 23 24 27 28 32 33 38 39. ...A) 45 46 B) 45 52 C) 44 45 D) 44 49 E) 40 46

HINTS FOR QUESTIONS 11 THROUGH 18.

11. ALTERNATING SERIES: 5 6↑7 8↑9 ?↑
                                    20 19   ?

12. ALTERNATING SERIES: 9 10↑11 12↑13 ?↑
                                         1   2   ?

13. INCREASES ALTERNATELY BY 2 (PLUS 2) THEN 3 (PLUS 3) *4* (PLUS 2) *6* (PLUS 3) *9* (PLUS 2) *11* (PLUS 3) *14* (PLUS 2) *16* (PLUS 3) *19* (PLUS 2) ? (PLUS 3) ?

14. ALTERNATING SERIES: 8 8↑10 10↑12 ?↑
                                     1   3   ?

15. ALTERNATING SERIES: 14↑↑15↑↑16↑ ↑
                                12   34   ??

16. ALTERNATING SERIES: 10 12↑15 17↑20 ?↑
                                    50   50   ?

17. ALTERNATING SERIES: 1 2 3↑4 5 6↑7 8 ?↑
                                      50   51   ?

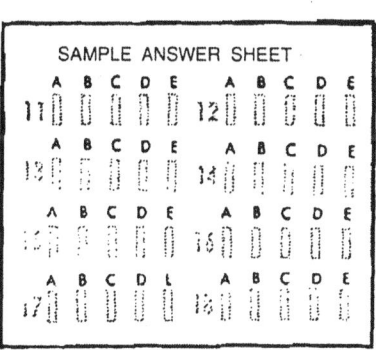

18. INCREASES ALTERNATELY BY (PLUS 1), (PLUS 2), (PLUS 1), (PLUS 3), (PLUS 1), (PLUS 4), ETC. -20 (PLUS 1) 21 (PLUS 2) 23 (PLUS 1) 24 (PLUS 3) 27 (PLUS 1) 28 (PLUS 4) 32 (PLUS 1) 33 (PLUS 5) 38 (PLUS 1) 39 (PLUS 6) ? (PLUS 1) ?

THE CORRECT ANSWERS TO THE SAMPLE QUESTIONS ABOVE ARE: 11A, 12C, 13A, 14B, 15D, 16D, 17B, AND 18A.

NUMBER SERIES-PRACTICE
TEST 1

DO FIRST THOSE QUESTIONS THAT YOU CAN DO EASILY. THEN GO BACK AND DO THE ONES THAT YOU SKIPPED.

Work *20 minutes* on this test. No more. No less. If you finish before the 20 minutes are up, go over your answers again. Mark your answers on the Answer Sheet on the next page.

#	Series	A	B	C	D	E
1.	10 11 12 10 11 12 10	10 11	12 10	11 10	11 12	10 12
2.	4 6 7 4 6 7 4	6 7	4 7	7 6	7 4	6 8
3.	7 7 3 7 7 4 7	4 5	4 7	5 7	7 5	7 7
4.	3 4 10 5 6 10 7	10 8	9 8	8 14	8 9	8 10
5.	6 6 7 7 8 8 9	10 11	10 10	9 10	9 9	10 9
6.	3 8 9 4 9 10 5	6 10	10 11	9 10	11 6	10 6
7.	2 4 3 6 4 8 5	6 10	10 7	10 6	9 6	6 7
8.	11 5 9 7 7 9 5	11 3	7 9	7 11	9 7	3 7
9.	12 10 8 8 6 7 4	2 2	6 4	6 2	4 6	2 6
10.	20 22 22 19 21 21 18	22 22	19 19	20 20	20 17	19 17
11.	5 7 6 10 7 13 8	16 9	16 10	9 15	10 15	15 9
12.	13 10 11 15 12 13 17	18 14	18 15	15 16	14 15	15 18
13.	30 27 24 21 18 15 12	9 3	9 6	6 3	12 9	8 5
14.	3 7 10 5 8 10 7	10 11	10 5	10 9	10 10	9 10
15.	12 4 13 6 14 8 15	10 17	17 10	10 12	16 10	10 16
16.	21 8 18 20 7 17 19	16 18	18 6	6 16	5 15	6 18
17.	14 16 16 18 20 20 22	22 24	26 28	24 26	24 24	24 28
18.	5 6 8 9 12 13 17	18 23	13 18	18 22	23 24	18 19
19.	1 3 5 5 2 4 6 6 3	7 4	5 5	1 3	5 7	7 7
20.	12 24 15 25 18 26 21	27 22	24 22	29 24	27 27	27 24
21.	17 15 21 18 10 16 19	20 5	5 11	11 11	11 20	15 14
22.	12 16 10 14 8 12 6	10 14	10 8	10 4	4 10	4 2
23.	13 4 5 13 6 7 13	13 8	8 13	8 9	8 8	7 8
24.	10 10 9 11 11 10 12	13 14	12 11	13 13	12 12	12 13

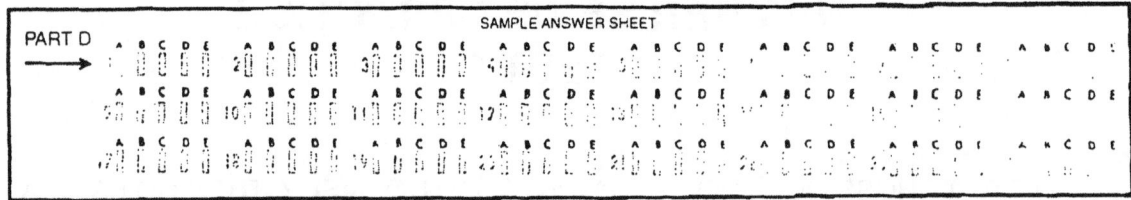

Now check your answers by comparing them with the correct answers shown below.

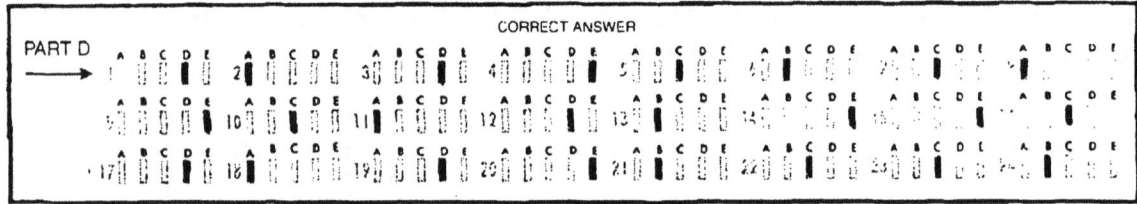

Count how many you got right, and write that number on this line ⟶ _____
(This is your Test Score.)

Meaning of Test Score
    If your Test Score is *17 or more,* you have a Good score.
    If your Test Score *is from 12 to 16,* you have a Fair score.
    If your Test Score is *11 or less,* you are not doing too well.

NUMBER SERIES-PRACTICE TEST 2

Do first those questions that you can do easily. Then go back and do the ones that you skipped.

Work *20 minutes* on this test. No more. No less. If you finish before the 20 minutes are up, go over your answers again. Mark your answers on the Answer Sheet on the next page.

1. 8 9 9 8 10 10 8 .... A) 11 8 B) 8 13 C) 8 11 D) 11 11 E) 8 8
2. 10 10 11 11 12 12 13 .... A) 15 15 B) 13 13 C) 14 14 D) 13 14 E) 14 15
3. 6 6 10 6 6 12 6 .... A) 6 14 B) 13 6 C) 14 6 D) 6 13 E) 6 6
4. 17 11 5 16 10 4 15 .... A) 13 9 B) 13 11 C) 8 5 D) 9 5 E) 9 3
5. 1 3 2 4 3 5 4 .... A) 6 8 B) 5 6 C) 6 5 D) 3 4 E) 3 5
6. 11 11 10 12 11 11 13 .... A) 12 14 B) 14 12 C) 14 14 D) 13 14 E) 13 12
7. 18 5 6 18 7 8 18 .... A) 9 9 B) 9 10 C) 18 9 D) 8 9 E) 18 7
8. 7 8 9 13 10 11 12 14 13 14. .. A) 15 16 B) 13 15 C) 14 15 D) 15 15 E) 13 14
                                           A) 15 16 B) 15 17 C) 14 17 D) 15 30 E) 30 17
9. 5 7 30 9 11 30 13 ....
10. 5 7 11 13 17 19 23 .... A) 27 29 B) 25 29 C) 25 27 D) 27 31 E) 29 31
11. 9 15 10 17 12 19 15 21 19 ..... A) 23 24 B) 25 23 C) 17 23 D) 23 31 E) 21 24
12. 34 37 30 33 26 29 22 .... A) 17 8 B) 18 11 C) 25 28 D) 25 20 B) 25 18
13. 10 16 12 14 14 12 16 .... A) 14 12 B) 10 18 C) 10 14 D) 14 18 E) 14 16
14. 11 12 18 11 13 19 11 14 .... A) 18 11 B) 16 11 C) 20 11 D) 11 21 E) 17 11
15. 20 9 8 19 10 9 18 11 10 .... A) 19 11 B) 17 10 C) 19 12 D) 17 12 E) 19 10
16. 28 27 26 31 30 29 34 .... A) 36 32 B) 32 31 C) 33 32 D) 33 36 E) 35 36

17. 10 16 14 20 18 24 22 .... A) 28 32 B) 27 26 C) 28 26 D) 26 28 E) 27 28
18. 9 9 7 8 7 7 9 10 5 .... A) 5 11 B) 11 12 C) 5 9 D) 9 11 E) 5 5
19. 5 7 11 17 10 12 16 22 15 17 . A) 27 26 B) 19 23 C) 19 27 D) 21 23 E) 21 27
20. 12 19 13 20 14 21 15 .... A) 16 17 B) 22 16 C) 16 22 D) 15 22 E) 15 16
21. 6 6 8 10 10 12 14 .... A) 14 14 B) 14 16 C) 16 16 D) 12 14 E) 10 10
22. 8 1 9 3 10 5 11 .... A) 7 12 B) 6 12 C) 12 6 D) 7 8 E) 6 7
23. 30 11 24 12 19 14 15 17 12
    21 10 .... A) 23 8 B) 25 8 C) 26 9 D) 24 9 E) 25 9
24. 24 30 29 22 28 27 19 26 25
    15 24 .... A) 14 23 B) 19 18 C) 23 22 D) 25 11 E) 23 10

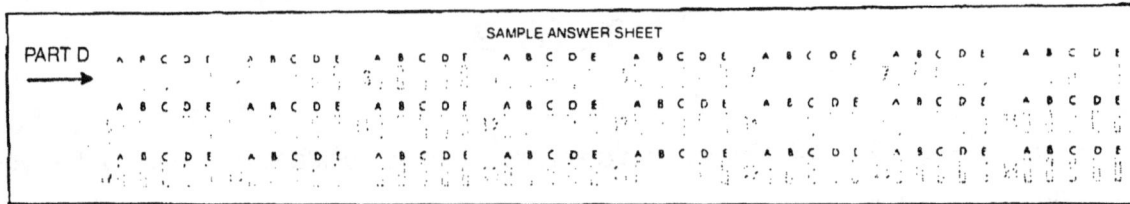

Now check your answers by comparing them with the correct answers shown below.

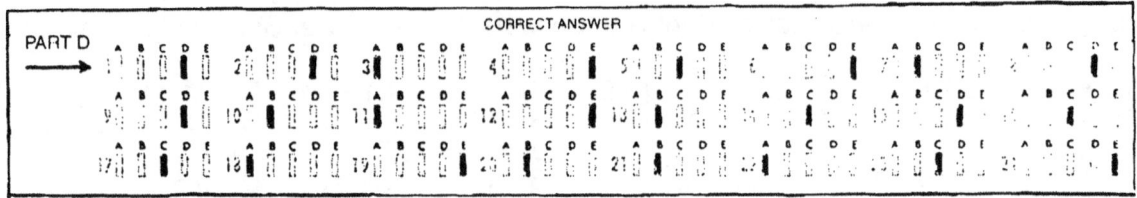

Count how many you got right, and write that number on this line ⟶ _____
(This is your Test Score.)

Meaning of Test Score
    If your Test Score is *17 or more,* you have a Good score.
    If your Test Score *is from 12 to 16,* you have a Fair score.
    If your Test Score is *11 or less,* you are not doing too well.

NUMBER SERIES-PRACTICE
TEST 3

Do first those questions that you can do easily. Then go back and do the ones that you skipped.

Work *20 minutes* on this test. No more. No less. If you finish before the 20 minutes are up, go over your answers again. Mark your answers on the Sample Answer Sheet on the next page.

		A)	B)	C)	D)	E)
1.	13 12 8 11 10 8 9	8 7	6 8	8 6	8 8	7 8
2.	13 18 13 17 13 16 13	15 13	13 14	13 15	14 15	15 14
3.	13 13 10 12 12 10 11	10 10	10 9	11 9	9 11	11 10
4.	6 5 4 6 5 4 6	4 6	6 4	5 4	5 6	4 5
5.	10 10 9 8 8 7 6	5 5	5 4	6 5	6 4	5 3
6.	20 16 18 14 16 12 14	16 12	10 12	16 18	12 12	12 10
7.	7 12 8 11 9 10 10	11 9	9 8	9 11	10 11	9 10
8.	13 13 12 15 15 14 17	17 16	14 17	16 19	19 19	16 16
9.	19 18 12 17 16 13 15	16 12	14 14	12 14	14 12	12 16
10.	7 15 12 8 16 13 9	17 14	17 10	14 10	14 17	10 14
11.	18 15 6 16 14 6 14	12 6	14 13	6 12	13 12	13 6
12.	6 6 5 8 8 7 10 10	8 12	9 12	12 12	12 9	9 9
13.	17 20 23 26 29 32 35	37 40	41 44	38 41	38 42	36 39
14.	15 5 7 16 9 11 17	18 13	15 17	12 19	13 15	12 13
15.	19 17 16 16 13 15 10	14 7	12 9	14 9	7 12	10 14
16.	11 1 16 10 6 21 9	12 26	26 8	11 26	11 8	8 11
17.	21 21 19 17 17 15 13	11 11	13 11	11 9	9 7	13 13
18.	23 22 20 19 16 15 11	6 5	10 9	6 1	10 6	10 5
19.	17 10 16 9 14 8 11	7 11	7 7	10 4	4 10	7 4
20.	11 9 14 12 17 15 20 18 23	21 24	26 21	21 26	24 27	26 29
21.	7 5 9 7 11 9 13	11 14	10 15	11 15	12 14	10 14
22.	9 10 11 7 8 9 5	6 7	7 8	5 6	6 4	7 5
23.	8 9 10 10 9 10 11 11 10 11 12	11 12	12 10	11 11	12 11	11 13
24.	5 6 8 9 12 13 17 18 23 24	30 31	25 31	29 30	25 30	30 37

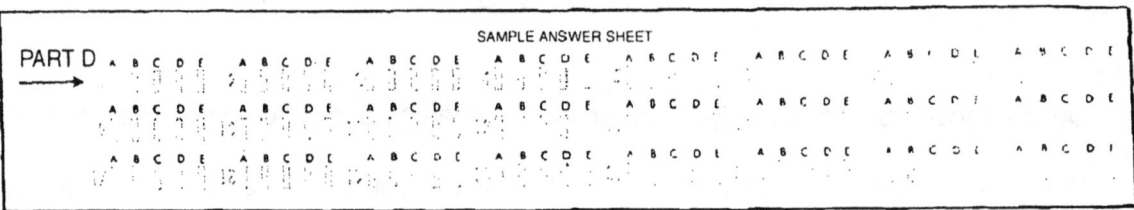

Now check your answers by comparing them with the correct answers shown below.

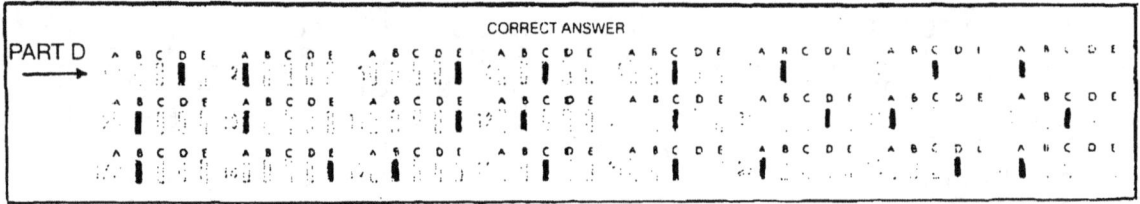

Count how many you got right, and write that number on this line ⟶ _____
(This is your Test Score.)

Meaning of Test Score
    If your Test Score is *17 or more,* you have a Good score.
    If your Test Score *is from 12 to 16,* you have a Fair score.
    If your Test Score is *11 or less,* you are not doing too well.

CLERK-CARRIER EXAMINATION

WHAT IS IN THE EXAMINATION

The test for Clerk-Carrier has four parts. They are:

- Part A: Address Checking
  How quickly can you spot whether two addresses are alike or different? This test is harder than the one for the Mail Handler. See practice questions and tests.

- Part B: Memory for Addresses
  How well can you memorize several groups of names and locations? See practice questions and test.

- Part C: Word Meaning and Reading
  Word Meaning: How well do you understand words you might have to read on the job? See practice questions and test.
  Reading: How well do you understand the meaning of paragraphs that you are asked to read? See practice questions and tests.

- Part D: Number Series
  How well can you discover the relationship between numbers in a series? See practice questions and tests.

After you have passed this test, you will be placed on a list of eligible on the basis of your score. If you are entitled to veterans' preference, you will be given the extra credit. (The higher your score, the nearer the top of the list you will be.)

NOTE:
The full written test for the Clerk-Carrier examination consists of the four (4) parts listed above. However, in recent years, the United States Postal Service, in accordance with staffing needs and conditions, has been offering only three of these parts on the Clerk-Carrier written examination. Therefore, be sure to check the Official Announcement before you take your test.

Study only the sections in this book on which you will be tested. If all four, study the entire book. If three, study only those three sections.

2

PRACTICE TESTS

HOW TO USE THESE PRACTICE TESTS

On the following pages, you will find questions just like the ones used in the Civil Service examinations for these jobs in the post office. Each type of question is explained separately. Study the sample and then do the practice tests.

Each practice test is timed. Have a friend watch the time for you.

When you have finished each practice test, go back and check your answers to find out what your score is. Then compare your score with the scale that goes with the test to determine how well you did. This will help you to find out where you need more practice.

Be sure to do the practice tests before you attempt the sample tests at the back. These tests are exactly like the ones you will have to take in the examinations. The time limit for each part and the types of questions in each part are exactly like they are in the Civil Service examinations.

SAMPLE CLERK-CARRIER TEST

Now that you have studied the instructions and taken the practice tests in this book, you are ready to take the Sample Tests. There is one Sample Test for Clerk-Carrier.

The Sample Tests are exactly like the ones you will have to take in the examinations. The time allowances and the numbers of questions are the same as they are in the real tests.

At the back of the book you will find some answer sheets to use. These answer sheets are like the ones you will use in the examinations.

When you are ready to try a Sample Test, tear out an answer sheet from the back of the book. Then do what the instructions tell you to do. Remember that in the address-checking and memory for addresses sections you will lose credit for wrong answers. In the address-checking section it will be better not to guess.

After you have finished answering the questions for a sample test, compare your answers with the correct answers for that test and see how well you did.

Clerk-Carrier Test

Time Required for Each Part
- Part A
  - Samples — 3 minutes
  - Test — 6 minutes
- Part B
  - Samples and Study — 6 minutes (Approximately)
  - Test—List 1 Practice — 3 minutes
  - Test—List 2 Practice — 3 minutes
  - Study — 5 minutes
  - Test—List 1 — 5 minutes
  - Test—List 2 — 5 minutes
- Part C
  - Samples — 3 minutes
  - Test — 30 minutes
- Part D
  - Samples — 20 minutes (Approximately)
  - Test — 30 minutes

INTERPRETATION OF TEST SCORES ON SAMPLE CLERK–CARRIER TEST

After you have taken a Part of the test or after you have finished the test, compare your answers with those given in the Correct Answers to Sample Test. You will find them on page 20.

For the Address Checking (Part A), count the number that you got right and the number that you got wrong. (If you didn't mark anything for a question, it doesn't get counted.)

    From the number right
    Subtract the number wrong
    This number (the difference) is your score⟶

The meaning of the score is as follows:

52 or higher	Good.
Between 32 and 51	Fair.
Below 32	You need more practice.

Go back and see where you made your mistakes. Were you careless? Did you work too slowly?

In the Memory for Addresses (Part B), only Test-List 2, which you recorded on your answer sheet, counts. For that Part, count the number that you got right and the number that you got wrong. (If you didn't mark anything for a question, it doesn't get counted.)

Divide the number wrong by 4. _____
    From the number right
    Subtract ¼ the number wrong
    This number (the difference) is your score⟶

The meaning of the score is as follows:

44 or higher	Good.
Between 26 and 43	Fair.
Below 26	You need more practice.

Go back and see where you made your mistakes. Were you careless? Did you work too slowly? Try to find out what is the best way for you to memorize.

For Word Meaning and Reading, your score is the number right: _____.

The meaning of the score is as follows:

24 or higher	Good.
Between 20 and 23	Fair.
Below 20	You need more study.

Go back and see where you made your mistakes. Were you careless? Did you spend too much time on the questions that were hard for you? Were there words that you didn't know? If you didn't know the words, try to build up your vocabulary. Some ways of doing this are suggested on page 58.

For Number Series (Part D), your score is the number right: _____.

The meaning of the score is as follows:

17 or higher	Good.
Between 12 and 16	Fair.
Below 12	You need more practice.

Go back and see why you didn't get a higher score. Did you make arithmetic mistakes? Were you careless? Did you have trouble finding the rule? If you did, keep working with the questions until you find the rules. See the suggestions given. Sometimes it helps to leave a question that is bothering you and go on and work on the others. Then come back to the ones you had to leave.

In the Clerk-Carrier test your scores on vocabulary, reading, and number series will be added together in order to get your score on the general abilities section of the test.

SAMPLE CLERK-CARRIER TEST

There are four parts to this test. It is best to have a friend to watch the time for you. The correct time limit for each part is given on page 1. Be careful not to take any more time than given in the instructions for each part.

Tear out an answer sheet from the back of the book and use it to mark your answers for each part of this test.

Directions and Samples for Part A

In this Part you will be given addresses to compare. On your answer sheet darken the box under A if the two addresses are exactly *Alike* in every way. Darken the box under D if they are *Different*.

Here are some sample questions for you to do. Mark your answers to them on the Sample Answer Sheet on this page. You should not take more than *3 minutes* to read and study the material on this page of the test.

Show your answer to a question by darkening completely the box corresponding to the letter that is the same as the letter of your answer. You must keep your mark within the box. If you have to erase a mark, be sure to erase it completely. Mark only one answer for each question.

1 ... 2134 S 20th St   2134 S 20th St

    Since the two addresses are exactly alike, mark A for question 1 on the Sample Answer Sheet.

2 ... 4608 N Warnock St   4806 N Warnock St
3 ... 1202 W Girard Dr   1202 W Girard Rd
4 ... Chappaqua N Y 10514   Chappaqua N Y 10514
5 ... 2207 Markland Ave   2207 Markham Ave

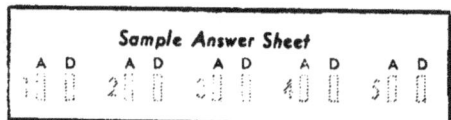

Now compare your answers with the Correct Answers to Sample Questions. If your answers are not the same as the correct answers shown, go back and study the samples to see where you made a mistake.

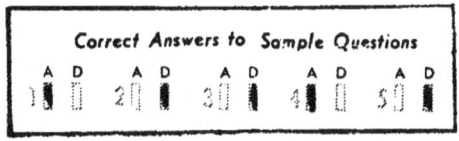

It will be to your advantage to work as quickly and accurately as possible since your score on this part of the test will be based on the number of wrong answers as well as the number of right answers. It is not expected that you will be able to finish all the questions in the time allowed.

Be sure to use a pencil so that you can make erasures.

Look at your answer sheet. The answers to this part of the examination must be marked in Part A of the answer sheet. Notice also that the answer spaces are numbered across the page. Mark the answer for question 1 in space 1.

When you begin the test, work as fast as you can without making mistakes. Do as many questions as you can in the time allowed.

You will have *6 minutes* to answer as many of the 95 questions as you can.

DO NOT TURN THIS PAGE UNTIL YOU ARE READY TO BEGIN THE TEST.

PART A

REMEMBER: Mark your answers on the separate answer sheet. Use "A" for "Alike" and "D" for "Different." Work as quickly as you can.

1 ...	405 Winter Rd NW	405 Winter Rd NW
2 ...	607 S Calaveras Rd	607 S Calaveras Rd
3 ...	8406 La Casa St	8406 La Cosa St
4 ...	121 N Rippon St	121 N Rippon St
5 ...	Wideman Ark	Wiseman Ark
6 ...	Sodus NY 14551	Sodus NY 14551
7 ...	3429 Hermosa Dr	3429 Hermoso Dr
8 ...	3628 S Zeeland St	3268 S Zeeland St
9 ...	1330 Cheverly Ave NE	1330 Cheverly Ave NE
10 ...	1689 N Derwood Dr	1689 N Derwood Dr
11 ...	3886 Sunrise Ct	3886 Sunrise Ct
12 ...	635 La Calle Mayor	653 La Calle Mayor
13 ...	2560 Lansford Pl	2560 Lansford St
14 ...	4631 Central Ave	4631 Central Ave
15 ...	Mason City Iowa 50401	Mason City Iowa 50401
16 ...	758 Los Arboles Ave SE	758 Los Arboles Ave SW
17 ...	3282 E Downington St	3282 E Dunnington St
18 ...	7117 N Burlingham Ave	7117 N Burlingham Ave
19 ...	32 Oaklawn Blvd	32 Oakland Blvd
20 ...	1274 Manzana Rd	1274 Manzana Rd
21 ...	4598 E Kenilworth Dr	4598 E Kenilworth Dr
22 ...	Dayton Okla 73449	Dagton Okla 73449
23 ...	1172 W 83rd Ave	1127 W 83rd Ave
24 ...	6434 E Pulaski St	6434 E Pulaski Ct
25 ...	2764 N Rutherford Pl	2764 N Rutherford Pl
26 ...	565 Greenville Blvd SE	565 Greenview Blvd SE
27 ...	Washington D C 20013	Washington D C 20018
28 ...	3824 Massasoit St	3824 Massasoit St
29 ...	22 Sagnaw Pkwy	22 Saganaw Pkwy
30 ...	Byram Conn 10573	Byram Conn 10573
31 ...	1928 S Fairfield Ave	1928 S Fairfield St
32 ...	36218 Overhills Dr	36218 Overhills Dr
33 ...	516 Avenida de Las Americas NW	516 Avenida de Las Americas NW
34 ...	7526 Naraganset Pl SW	7526 Naraganset Pl SW
35 ...	52626 W Ogelsby Dr	52626 W Ogelsby Dr
36 ...	1003 Winchester Rd	1003 Westchester Rd
37 ...	3478 W Cavanaugh Ct	3478 W Cavenaugh Ct
38 ...	Kendall Calif 90551	Kendell Calif 90551
39 ...	225 El Camino Blvd	225 El Camino Ave
40 ...	7310 Via de los Pisos	7310 Via de los Pinos
41 ...	1987 Wellington Ave SW	1987 Wellington Ave SW
42 ...	3124 S 71st St	3142 S 71st St
43 ...	729 Lincolnwood Blvd	729 Lincolnwood Blvd
44 ...	1166 N Beaumont Dr	1166 S Beaumont Dr
45 ...	3224 W Winecona Pl	3224 W Winecona Pl
46 ...	608 La Calle Bienvenida	607 La Calle Bienvenida
47 ...	La Molte Iowa 52045	La Molte Iowa 52045

GO ON TO NUMBER 48 ON THE NEXT PAGE.

48	8625 Armitage Ave NW	8625 Armitage Ave NW
49	2343 Broadview Ave	2334 Broadview Ave
50	4279 Sierra Grande Ave NE	4279 Sierra Grande Dr NE
51	165 32d Ave	165 32d Ave
52	12742 N Deerborn St	12724 N Deerborn St
53	114 Estancia Ave	141 Estancia Ave
54	351 S Berwyn Rd	351 S Berwyn Pl
55	7732 Avenida Manana SW	7732 Avenida Manana SW
56	6337 C St SW	6337 G St SW
57	57895 E Drexyl Ave	58795 E Drexyl Ave
58	Altro Tex 75923	Altra Tex 75923
59	3465 S Nashville St	3465 N Nashville St
60	1226 Odell Blvd NW	1226 Oddell Blvd NW
61	94002 Chappel Ct	94002 Chappel Ct
62	512 La Vega Dr	512 La Veta Dr
63	8774 W Winona Pl	8774 E Winona Pl
64	6431 Ingleside St SE	6431 Ingleside St SE
65	2270 N Leanington St	2270 N Leanington St
66	235 Calle de Los Vecinos	235 Calle de Los Vecinos
67	3987 E Westwood Ave	3987 W Westwood Ave
68	Skamokawa Wash	Skamohawa Wash
69	2674 E Champlain Cir	2764 E Champlain Cir
70	8751 Elmhurst Blvd	8751 Elmwood Blvd
71	6649 Solano Dr	6649 Solana Dr
72	4423 S Escenaba St	4423 S Escenaba St
73	1198 N St NW	1198 M St NW
74	Sparta Ga	Sparta Va
75	96753 Wrightwood Ave	96753 Wrightwood Ave
76	2445 Sangamow Ave SE	2445 Sangamow Ave SE
77	5117 E 67 Pl	5171 E 67 Pl
78	847 Mesa Grande Pl	847 Mesa Grande Ct
79	1100 Cermaken St	1100 Cermaker St
80	321 Tijeras Ave NW	321 Tijeras Ave NW
81	3405 Prospect St	3405 Prospect St
82	6643 Burlington Pl	6643 Burlingtown Pl
83	851 Esperanza Blvd	851 Esperanza Blvd
84	Jenkinjones W Va	Jenkinjones W Va
85	1008 Pennsylvania Ave SE	1008 Pennsylvania Ave SW
86	2924 26th St N	2929 26th St N
87	7115 Highland Dr	7115 Highland Dr
88	Chaptico Md	Chaptica Md
89	3508 Camron Mills Rd	3508 Camron Mills Rd
90	67158 Capston Dr	67158 Capston Dr
91	3613 S Taylor Ave	3631 S Taylor Ave
92	2421 Menokin Dr	2421 Menokin Dr
93	3226 M St NW	3226 N St NW
94	1201 S Court House Rd	1201 S Court House Rd
95	Findlay Ohio 45840	Findley Ohio 45840

STOP.

**If you finish before the time is up, check your answers for Part A.
Do not go to any other part.**

When the time is up, turn to page 6.

Samples for Part B

Part B has five boxes labeled A, B, C, D, and E. Each box contains five addresses. Three of the five addresses are groups of street addresses like 2100–2799 Mall, 4800–4999 Cliff and 1900–2299 Laurel, and two are names of places. They are different in each box. You will be given two lists of addresses. For each street address or name in the list, you are to decide in which lettered box (A, B, C, D, or E) it belongs and then mark that box on the answer sheet. For List 1, the boxes will be shown on the same page with the addresses. While you are working on List 2, you will not be able to look at the boxes. Then you will have to match the addresses with the correct box from memory. Try to memorize the location of as many addresses as you can.

A	B	C	D	E
2100–2799 Mall Ceres 4800–4999 Cliff Natoma 1900–2299 Laurel	3900–4399 Mall Cedar 4000–4299 Cliff Foster 2300–2999 Laurel	4400–4599 Mall Niles 3300–3999 Cliff Dexter 3200–3799 Laurel	3400–3899 Mall Cicero 4500–4799 Cliff Pearl 3000–3199 Laurel	2800–3399 Mall Delhi 4300–4499 Cliff Magnet 1500–1899 Laurel

Sample Questions:

1. 3300–3999 Cliff—This address is in box C. So you would darken box C.
2. Natoma—This name is in box A. So you would darken box A.
3. Foster
4. 1500–1899 Laurel
5. 3900–4399 Mall
6. Pearl
7. 3200–3799 Laurel

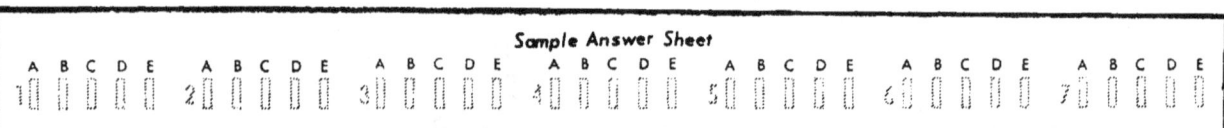

The answers to samples 3 to 7 are: 3B, 4E, 5B, 6D, and 7C.

In List 1 the boxes with the addresses will be before your eyes. Therefore you will be able to check your answers by looking at the top of the page. However, checking takes time and the more you remember, the faster you will be able to work. On List 2 the boxes with the addresses will *not* be shown. Then you will have only your memory to depend on when answering the questions. Thus, memory will be very important in this test.

Different people study in different ways. Many people find it easier to learn the addresses in one box at a time than to learn all the addresses at once.

You will now have *3 minutes* to study the addresses and letters so that you will have a good idea of the letter that goes with each address. Do not spend more than 3 minutes studying the addresses.

Now memorize the addresses in the boxes. These are the addresses that will be in the test. TRY TO LEARN THE LOCATION OF AS MANY ADDRESSES AS YOU CAN. Cover each box with your hand and see if you can repeat, to yourself, the addresses in that box.

DO NOT TURN THIS PAGE UNTIL THE TIME IS UP. THEN TURN TO PAGE 7.

PART B

List 1

For each question, mark the top answer sheet on the next page to show the letter of the box in which the address belongs. Try to remember the location of as many addresses as you can. You will now have *3 minutes* for List 1. If you are not sure of an answer you should guess.

A	B	C	D	E
2100–2799 Mall Ceres 4800–4999 Cliff Natoma 1900–2299 Laurel	3900–4399 Mall Cedar 4000–4299 Cliff Foster 2300–2999 Laurel	4400–4599 Mall Niles 3300–3999 Cliff Dexter 3200–3799 Laurel	3400–3899 Mall Cicero 4500–4799 Cliff Pearl 3000–3199 Laurel	2800–3399 Mall Delhi 4300–4499 Cliff Magnet 1500–1899 Laurel

1. Magnet
2. Niles
3. 3400–3899 Mall
4. 1900–2299 Laurel
5. Cicero
6. Dexter
7. 2300–2999 Laurel
8. 3300–3999 Cliff

9. 3200–3799 Laurel
10. 2100–2799 Mall
11. Pearl
12. 3200–3799 Laurel
13. Ceres
14. 4500–4799 Cliff
15. 3900–4399 Mall
16. Delhi

17. 4300–4499 Cliff
18. 3000–3199 Laurel
19. Ceres
20. Foster
21. Natoma
22. 4400–4599 Mall
23. Cedar
24. 2300–2999 Laurel

25. 1500–1899 Laurel
26. 4000–4299 Cliff
27. Dexter
28. Magnet
29. 3300–3999 Cliff
30. 3400–3899 Mall
31. Niles
32. 2100–2799 Mall

33. 1900–2299 Laurel
34. Cedar
35. Pearl
36. 2800–3399 Mall
37. 4800–4999 Cliff
38. 3900–4399 Mall
39. Foster
40. 3000–3199 Laurel

41. Ceres
42. Niles
43. 3400–3899 Mall
44. Delhi
45. 2300–2999 Laurel
46. 4500–4799 Cliff
47. Dexter
48. Magnet

49. 3300–3999 Cliff
50. Cicero
51. 4300–4499 Cliff
52. 3900–4399 Mall
53. Natoma
54. 3200–3799 Laurel
55. Pearl
56. 4000–4299 Cliff

57. 4500–4799 Cliff
58. 2100–2799 Mall
59. Foster
60. 4400–4599 Mall
61. 4800–4999 Cliff
62. Ceres
63. 2800–3399 Mall
64. 1500–1899 Laurel

65. Natoma
66. 3000–3199 Laurel
67. 4000–4299 Cliff
68. Niles
69. 2300–2999 Laurel
70. Magnet
71. Delhi
72. 4400–4599 Mall

73. Cicero
74. Cedar
75. 2800–3399 Mall
76. 1900–2299 Laurel
77. Dexter
78. Pearl
79. 4300–4499 Cliff
80. 3900–4399 Mall

81. Foster
82. 4800–4999 Cliff
83. Delhi
84. Ceres
85. 1500–1899 Laurel
86. Natoma
87. 2800–3399 Mall
88. Niles

STOP.

If you finish before the time is up, go back and check your answers for the questions on this page. Do not go to any other page until the time is up.

List 2

For each question, mark the answer sheet on the next page to show the letter of the box in which the address belongs. If you are not sure of an answer, you should guess. You will record your answers on the next page. While you are working on List 2, do not turn to any other page. You will have *3 minutes* to do this list.

1. Cedar	25. 4800–4999 Cliff	49. 4500–4799 Cliff	73. 4000–4299 Cliff
2. 4300–4499 Cliff	26. 1500–1899 Laurel	50. 1900–2299 Laurel	74. 3400–3899 Mall
3. 4400–4599 Mall	27. Cedar	51. Niles	75. 1900–2299 Laurel
4. Natoma	28. 4400–4599 Mall	52. 3300–3999 Cliff	76. 2800–3399 Mall
5. 2300–2999 Laurel	29. 4500–4799 Cliff	53. 2800–3399 Mall	77. Ceres
6. 4500–4799 Cliff	30. Dexter	54. Cicero	78. Magnet
7. Ceres	31. 3000–3199 Laurel	55. Delhi	79. Cicero
8. 3400–3899 Mall	32. Niles	56. 4000–4299 Cliff	80. 3200–3799 Laurel
9. Delhi	33. Delhi	57. Dexter	81. 3000–3199 Laurel
10. Dexter	34. 3900–4399 Mall	58. Magnet	82. 3900–4399 Mall
11. 1900–2299 Laurel	35. Cicero	59. 3000–3199 Laurel	83. Natoma
12. 3300–3999 Cliff	36. Dexter	60. 3900–4399 Mall	84. 3300–3999 Cliff
13. Cicero	37. 4800–4999 Cliff	61. Natoma	85. 3400–3899 Mall
14. 4000–4299 Cliff	38. 2300–2999 Laurel	62. 3000–3199 Laurel	86. Foster
15. 2100–2799 Mall	39. 2100–2799 Mall	63. 4300–4499 Cliff	87. 2100–2799 Mall
16. Foster	40. 3300–3999 Cliff	64. Cedar	88. 4300–4499 Cliff
17. Magnet	41. 3400–3899 Mall	65. 4400–4599 Mall	
18. Ceres	42. 4300–4499 Cliff	66. 1500–1899 Laurel	
19. 2800–3399 Mall	43. Ceres	67. 4800–4999 Cliff	
20. 3200–3799 Laurel	44. Foster	68. Delhi	
21. 4300–4499 Cliff	45. Magnet	69. Pearl	
22. Pearl	46. 3200–3799 Laurel	70. 2300–2999 Laurel	
23. 3900–4399 Mall	47. Pearl	71. 4500–4799 Cliff	
24. Natoma	48. 1500–1899 Laurel	72. Niles	

If you finish before the time is up, go back and check your answers to this part only. When the time is up turn back to page 6 and study the boxes again. You will have *5 minutes* to restudy the addresses. When that time is up, go on to page 7 and do that list again, using the bottom answer sheet on page 8. You will have *5 minutes* to do List 1 again. When that time is up turn to page 11 and read the instructions.

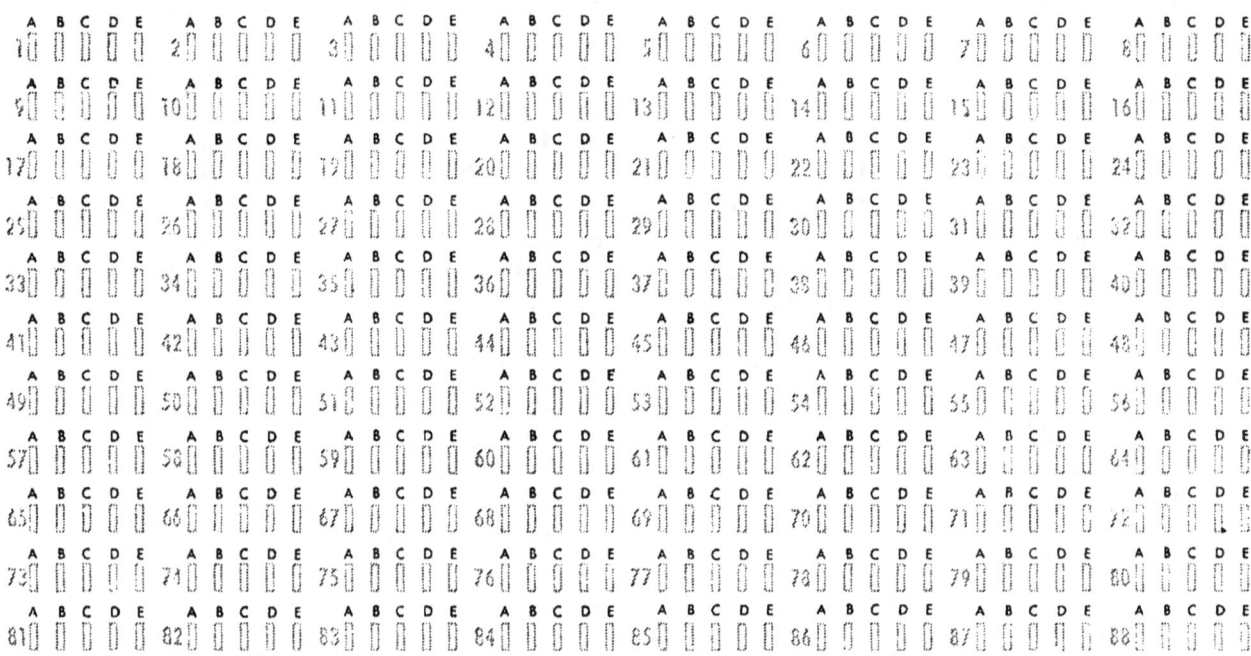

Test-List 2

For each question, mark your answer sheet to show the letter of the box in which the address belongs. Be sure to mark your answers on the answer sheet that you used for Part A. Your answers will go in the section labeled Part B. The first question is numbered 1. You will have *5 minutes* to do Test—List 2. During the 5 minutes for this list, do not turn to any other page.

1. Cedar
2. 4300–4499 Cliff
3. 4400–4599 Mall
4. Natoma
5. 2300–2999 Laurel
6. 4500–4799 Cliff
7. Ceres
8. 3400–3899 Mall

9. Delhi
10. Dexter
11. 1900–2299 Laurel
12. 3300–3999 Cliff
13. Cicero
14. 4000–4299 Cliff
15. 2100–2799 Mall
16. Foster

17. Magnet
18. Ceres
19. 2800–3399 Mall
20. 3200–3799 Laurel
21. 4300–4499 Cliff
22. Pearl
23. 3900–4399 Mall
24. Natoma

25. 4800–4999 Cliff
26. 1500–1899 Laurel
27. Cedar
28. 4400–4599 Mall
29. 4500–4799 Cliff
30. Dexter
31. 3000–3199 Laurel
32. Niles

33. Delhi
34. 3900–4399 Mall
35. Cicero
36. Dexter
37. 4800–4999 Cliff
38. 2300–2999 Laurel
39. 2100–2799 Mall
40. 3300–3999 Cliff

41. 3400–3899 Mall
42. 4300–4499 Cliff
43. Ceres
44. Foster
45. Magnet
46. 3200–3799 Laurel
47. Pearl
48. 1500–1899 Laurel

49. 4500–4799 Cliff
50. 1900–2299 Laurel
51. Niles
52. 3300–3999 Cliff
53. 2800–3399 Mall
54. Cicero
55. Delhi
56. 4000–4299 Cliff

57. Dexter
58. Magnet
59. 3000–3199 Laurel
60. 3900–4399 Mall
61. Natoma
62. 3000–3199 Laurel
63. 4300–4499 Cliff
64. Cedar

65. 4400–4599 Mall
66. 1500–1899 Laurel
67. 4800–4999 Cliff
68. Delhi
69. Pearl
70. 2300–2999 Laurel
71. 4500–4799 Cliff
72. Niles

73. 4000–4299 Cliff
74. 3400–3899 Mall
75. 1900–2299 Laurel
76. 2800–3399 Mall
77. Ceres
78. Magnet
79. Cicero
80. 3200–3799 Laurel

81. 3000–3199 Laurel
82. 3900–4399 Mall
83. Natoma
84. 3300–3999 Cliff
85. 3400–3899 Mall
86. Foster
87. 2100–2799 Mall
88. 4300–4499 Cliff

STOP.

If you finish before the time is up, go back and rework the questions on this page only.

WHEN THE TIME IS UP, TURN TO THE NEXT PAGE.

Samples for Part C

In this Part there are two kinds of questions. In some questions you will have to say what a word or group of words, that is in italics, means. In other questions you will have to read a paragraph and then answer the questions that follow.

You will have *3 minutes* to study and do the sample questions on this page. Now do the sample questions and mark your answers on the Sample Answer Sheet on this page.

1. The reports were *consolidated* by the secretary. *Consolidated* means most nearly
   A) combined
   B) concluded
   C) distributed
   D) protected
   E) weighed

In this question the word *consolidated* is in italics. So you are to decide which one of the suggested answers means most nearly the same as *consolidated*. "Combined" means most nearly the same as consolidated; so you should have darkened box A for question 1.

2. "Post Office clerks assigned to stamp-windows are directly responsible financially in the selling of postage. In addition, they are expected to have a thorough knowledge as to the acceptability of matter offered for mailing. Any information which they give out to the public must be accurate."

The paragraph best supports the statement that clerks assigned to stamp-window duty
   A) must account for stamps issued to them for sale
   B) have had long training in other post office work
   C) advise the public only on matters of official business
   D) must refer continuously to the sources of postal regulations
   E) inspect the contents of every package offered for mailing

The statement that is best supported by the paragraph is that "clerks assigned to stamp-window duty must account for stamps issued them for sale." So you should have darkened box A for question 2.

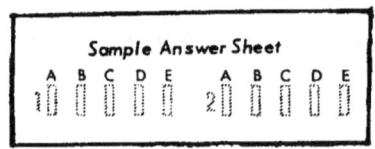

You will have *30 minutes* to do the 32 questions in this part.

DO NOT TURN THIS PAGE UNTIL THE 3 MINUTES FOR IT ARE UP.

PART C

In each of questions 1 through 20, choose the one of the five suggested answers that means most nearly the same as the word or group of words in italics.

Be sure to mark your answers for this part in Part C of the answer sheet.

1. The task *required* his attention. *Required* means most nearly
   A) held
   B) demanded
   C) aroused
   D) increased
   E) revived

2. Employees with previous training *assisted* the others. *Assisted* means most nearly
   A) instructed
   B) warned
   C) stimulated
   D) praised
   E) aided

3. He answered the question *hastily*. *Hastily* means most nearly
   A) incorrectly
   B) nervously
   C) indirectly
   D) bluntly
   E) quickly

4. The signs were *observable* to everyone. *Observable* means most nearly
   A) noticeable
   B) understandable
   C) acceptable
   D) agreeable
   E) available

5. The statements made in the article were *challenged*. *Challenged* means most nearly
   A) misunderstood
   B) disputed
   C) withdrawn
   D) expanded
   E) supported

6. A *trustworthy* messenger was needed to deliver the papers to the inspectors. *Trustworthy* means most nearly
   A) experienced
   B) cautious
   C) industrious
   D) capable
   E) dependable

7. They *endeavored* to keep the rate of production as high as it was when the machines were new. *Endeavor* means most nearly
   A) promised
   B) expected
   C) managed
   D) tried
   E) intended

8. The employee's *accomplishment* was unusually commendable. *Accomplishment* means most nearly
   A) solution
   B) achievement
   C) discovery
   D) proposal
   E) cooperation

9. She is *presumably* the only one who can help you. *Presumably* means most nearly
   A) undoubtedly
   B) practically
   C) probably
   D) reportedly
   E) possibly

10. It would be *advantageous* to begin this job first. *Advantageous* means most nearly
    A) proper
    B) profitable
    C) generous
    D) shrewd
    E) enterprising

11. The organization made a *deliberate* effort to conceal the facts. *Deliberate* means most nearly
    A) intentional
    B) impulsive
    C) desperate
    D) clever
    E) daring

12. The employee was *neglectful of* his responsibilities. *Neglectful of* means most nearly
    A) unworthy of
    B) inattentive to
    C) impatient about
    D) unhappy over
    E) unfit for

13. The foreman gave *specific* orders. *Specific* means most nearly
    A) precise
    B) brief
    C) urgent
    D) fundamental
    E) adequate

14. The procedure to be followed has been *sanctioned*. *Sanctioned* means most nearly
    A) publicly announced
    B) criticized
    C) officially authorized
    D) standardized
    E) carefully planned

15. He contradicted the statement *emphatically*. *Emphatically* means most nearly
    A) eagerly
    B) immediately
    C) positively
    D) reluctantly
    E) repeatedly

16. The trainees were given *minute* directions regarding the work. *Minute* means most nearly
    A) easy
    B) timely
    C) recorded
    D) numerous
    E) detailed

17. The news will bring a prompt *reaction*. *Reaction* means most nearly
    A) response
    B) outburst
    C) admission
    D) recommendation
    E) investigation

18. Only two of the members *participated* in the event. *Participated* means most nearly
    A) advanced
    B) took sides
    C) interfered
    D) took part
    E) argued

19. The facts he presented were *undeniable*. *Undeniable* means most nearly
    A) indefensible
    B) logical
    C) contestable
    D) justifiable
    E) indisputable

20. Attendance at safety lectures is *obligatory*. *Obligatory* means most nearly
    A) optional
    B) important
    C) inconvenient
    D) compulsory
    E) advisable

In each of questions 21 through 32 read the paragraph and then answer the question that follows it.

21. "Iron is used in making our bridges and skyscrapers, subways and steamships, railroads and automobiles, and nearly all kinds of machinery—besides millions of small articles varying from the farmer's scythe to the woman's needle."

    The paragraph best supports the statement that iron
    A) is the most abundant of the metals
    B) has many different uses
    C) is the strongest of all metals
    D) is the only material used in building skyscrapers and bridges
    E) is the most durable of the metals

22. "Some fire-resistant buildings, although wholly constructed of materials that will not burn, may be completely gutted by the spread of fire through their contents by way of hallways and other openings. They may even suffer serious structural damage by the collapse of metal beams and columns."

    The paragraph best supports the statement that some fire-resistant buildings
    A) suffer less damage from fire than from collapse of metal supports
    B) can be damaged seriously by fire
    C) have specially constructed halls and doors
    D) afford less protection to their contents than would ordinary buildings
    E) will burn readily

23. "Life is too short for one person to do very many things well. The person who determines fairly early what he can do that he likes to do, and who goes at it hard and stays with it, is likely to do the best work and find the most peace of mind."

    The paragraph best supports the statement that the reason the average man does not master many different jobs is that he
    A) desires peace of mind
    B) seldom has more than a few interests
    C) is unable to organize his ideas
    D) lacks the necessary time
    E) has a natural tendency to specialize

24. "Both the high school and the college should take the responsibility for preparing the student to get a job. Since the ability to write a good application letter is one of the first steps toward this goal, every teacher should be willing to do what he can to help the student learn to write such letters."

    The paragraph best supports the statement that
    A) inability to write a good letter often reduces one's job prospects
    B) the major responsibility of the school is to obtain jobs for its students
    C) success is largely a matter of the kind of work the student applies for first
    D) every teacher should teach a course in the writing of application letters
    E) letter writing is more important than most subjects taught in high schools and colleges

25. " 'White collar' is a term used to describe one of the largest groups of workers in American industry and trade. It distinguishes those who work with the pencil and the mind from those who depend on their hands and the machine. It suggests occupations in which physical exertion and handling of materials are not primary features of the job."

    The paragraph best supports the statement that "white collar" workers are
    A) the most powerful labor group because of their numbers
    B) not so strong physically as those who work with their hands
    C) those who supervise workers handling materials
    D) all whose work is entirely indoors
    E) not likely to use machines so much as are other groups of workers

26. "The location of a railway line is necessarily a compromise between the desire to build the line with as little expense as possible and the desire to construct it so that its route will cover that over which trade and commerce are likely to flow."

    The paragraph best supports the statement that the route selected for a railway line
    A) should be the one over which the line can be built most cheaply
    B) determines the location of commercial centers
    C) should always cover the shortest possible distance between its terminals
    D) cannot always be the one involving the lowest construction costs
    E) is determined chiefly by the kind of production in the area

27. "It is a common assumption that city directories are prepared and published by the cities concerned. However, the directory business is as much a private business as is the publishing of dictionaries and encyclopedias. The companies financing the publication make their profits through the sales of the directories themselves and through the advertising in them."

    The paragraph best supports the statement that
    A) the publication of a city directory is a commercial enterprise
    B) the size of a city directory limits the space devoted to advertising
    C) many city directories are published by dictionary and encyclopedia concerns
    D) city directories are sold at cost to local residents and businessmen
    E) the preparation of a city directory, but not the printing, is a responsibility of the local government

28. "A survey to determine the subjects that have helped students most in their jobs shows that typewriting leads all other subjects in the business group. It also leads among the subjects college students consider most valuable and would take again if they were to return to high school."

    The paragraph best supports the statement that
    A) the ability to type is an asset in business and in school
    B) students who return to night school take typing
    C) students with a knowledge of typing do superior work in college
    D) every person should know how to type
    E) success in business is assured those who can type

29. "Since duplicating machines are being changed constantly, the person who is in the market for such a machine should not purchase offhand the kind with which he is most familiar or the one recommended by the first salesman who calls on him. Instead he should analyze his particular equipment situation and then investigate all the possibilities."

The paragraph best supports the statement that, when duplicating equipment is being purchased,
A) the purchaser should choose equipment that he can use with the least extra training
B) the latest models should always be bought
C) the needs of the purchaser's office should determine the selection
D) the buyer should have his needs analyzed by an office-equipment salesman
E) the recommendations of salesmen should usually be ignored

30. "There has been a slump in first-aid training in the industries, and yet one should not fall into the error of thinking there is less interest in first aid in industry. The falling off has been in the number of new employees needing such training. It appears that in industries interested in first-aid training there is now actually a higher percentage so trained than there ever was before."

The paragraph best supports the statement that first-aid training is
A) a means of avoiding the more serious effects of accidents
B) being abandoned because of expense
C) helpful in every line of work
D) of great importance to employees
E) sometimes given new workers in industry

31. "There exists a false but popular idea that a clue is a mysterious fact which most people overlook but which some very keen investigator easily discovers and recognizes as having, in itself, a remarkable meaning. The clue is most often an ordinary fact which an observant person picks up—something which gains its significance when, after a long series of careful investigations, it is connected with a network of other clues."

The paragraph best supports the statement that to be of value clues must be
A) discovered by skilled investigators
B) found under mysterious circumstances
C) connected with other facts
D) discovered soon after the crime
E) observed many times

32. "It is wise to choose a duplicating machine that will do the work required with the greatest efficiency and at the least cost. Users with a large volume of business need speedy machines that cost little to operate and are well made."

The paragraph best supports the statement that
A) most users of duplicating machines prefer low operating cost to efficiency
B) a well-built machine will outlast a cheap one
C) a duplicating machine is not efficient unless it is sturdy
D) a duplicating machine should be both efficient and economical
E) in duplicating machines speed is more usual than low operating cost

STOP.

If you finish before the time is up, check your answers to Part C. Do not go to any other part.

WHEN THE TIME IS UP, TURN TO PAGE 17.

Samples for Part D

In each of the questions in this Part, there is at the left a series of numbers which follow some definite order and, at the right, five sets of two numbers each.

You are to look at the numbers in the series at the left and find out what order they follow. Then decide what the next two numbers in that series would be if the same order were continued. Next find these two numbers in one of the sets at the right, and darken the box on your answer sheet which has the same letter as the answer you select.

Samples

Now do sample question 1. Mark your answer in the space for question 1 on the Sample Answer Sheet on this page.

1. 1 2 3 4 5 6 7... A) 1 2 B) 5 6 C) 8 9 D) 4 5 E) 7 8

The numbers in this series are increasing by 1. If the series were continued for two more numbers, it would read: 1 2 3 4 5 6 7 8 9. Therefore the correct answer is 8 and 9, and you should have darkened C on the Sample Answer Sheet for question 1.

2. 15 14 13 12 11 10 9. . A) 2 1 B) 17 16 C) 8 9 D) 8 7 E) 9 8

The numbers in this series are decreasing by 1. If the series were continued for two more numbers, it would read: 15 14 13 12 11 10 9 8 7. Therefore the correct answer is 8 and 7, and you should have darkened D on the Sample Answer Sheet for question 2.

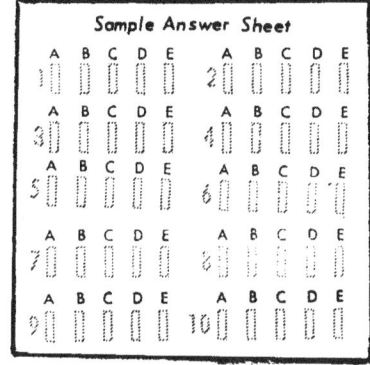

3. 20 20 21 21 22 22 23....... A) 23 23 B) 23 24 C) 19 19 D) 22 23 E) 21 22

Each number in this series is repeated and then increased by 1. If the series were continued for two more numbers, it would read: 20 20 21 21 22 22 23 23 24. Therefore the correct answer is 23 and 24, and you should have darkened B on the Sample Answer Sheet for question 3.

4. 17 3 17 4 17 5 17......... A) 6 17 B) 6 7 C) 17 6 D) 5 6 E) 17 7

This series is the number 17 separated by numbers increasing by 1, beginning with the number 3. If the series were continued for two more numbers, it would read: 17 3 17 4 17 5 17 6 17. Therefore the correct answer is 6 and 17, and you should have darkened A on the Sample Answer Sheet for question 4.

5. 1 2 4 5 7 8 10............. A) 11 12 B) 12 14 C) 10 13 D) 12 13 E) 11 13

The numbers in this series are increasing first by 1 (that is plus 1) and then by 2 (that is plus 2). If the series were continued for two more numbers, it would read: 1 2 4 5 7 8 10 (plus 1) which is *11* (plus 2) which is *13*. Therefore the correct answer is 11 and 13, and you should have darkened E on the Sample Answer Sheet for question 5.

Now you will have *10 minutes* to read and work sample questions 6 through 18. Mark your answers on the Sample Answer Sheets.

6. 21 21 20 20 19 19 18....... A) 18 18 B) 18 17 C) 17 18 D) 17 17 E) 18 19

7. 1 22 1 23 1 24 1........... A) 26 1 B) 25 26 C) 25 1 D) 1 26 E) 1 25

8. 1 20 3 19 5 18 7........... A) 8 9 B) 8 17 C) 17 10 D) 17 9 E) 9 18

9. 4 7 10 13 16 19 22......... A) 23 26 B) 25 27 C) 25 26 D) 25 28 E) 24 27

10. 30 2 28 4 26 6 24......... A) 23 9 B) 26 8 C) 8 9 D) 26 22 E) 8 22

Explanations for questions 6 through 10.

6. Each number in the series repeats itself and then decreases by 1 or minus 1; *21* (repeat) *21* (minus 1) which makes *20* (repeat) *20* (minus 1) which makes *19* (repeat) *19* (minus 1) which makes *18* (repeat) ? (minus 1) ?
7. The number 1 is separated by numbers which begin with 22 and increase by 1; *1 22 1* (increase 22 by 1) which makes *23 1* (increase 23 by 1) which makes *24 1* (increase 24 by 1) which makes ?
8. This is best explained by two alternating series—one series starts with *1* and increases by 2 or plus 2; the other series starts with *20* and decreases by 1 or minus 1.

    1 ↑ *3* ↑ *5* ↑ *7* ↑ ?
     20   *19* *18*   ?

9. This series of numbers increases by 3 (plus 3) beginning with the first number. *4* (plus 3) *7* (plus 3) *10* (plus 3) *13* (plus 3) *16* (plus 3) *19* (plus 3) *22* (plus 3) ? (plus 3) ?
10. Look for two alternating series—one series starts with 30 and decreases by 2 (minus 2), the other series starts with 2 and increases by 2 (plus 2).

    30 ↑ *28* ↑ *26* ↑ *24* ↑ ?
     2   *4*   *6*   ?

The correct answers to sample questions 6 through 10 are: 6B, 7C, 8D, 9D, and 10E.

Now try questions 11 to 18.

11. 5 6 20 7 8 19 9............... A) 10 18 B) 18 17 C) 10 17 D) 18 19 E) 10 11
12. 9 10 1 11 12 2 13............. A) 2 4   B) 3 14   C) 14 3   D) 14 15 E) 14 1
13. 4 6 9 11 14 16 19.............. A) 21 24 B) 22 25 C) 20 22 D) 21 23 E) 22 24
14. 8 8 1 10 10 3 12............... A) 13 13 B) 12 5   C) 12 4   D) 13 5   E) 4 12
15. 14 1 2 15 3 4 16................ A) 5 16   B) 6 7   C) 5 17   D) 5 6   E) 17 5
16. 10 12 50 15 17 50 20............ A) 50 21 B) 21 50 C) 50 22 D) 22 50 E) 22 24
17. 1 2 3 50 4 5 6 51 7 8........... A) 9 10   B) 9 52   C) 51 10 D) 10 52 E) 10 50
18. 20 21 23 24 27 28 32 33 38 39...... A) 45 46 B) 45 52 C) 44 45 D) 44 49 E) 40 46

Hints for questions 11 through 18.

11. Alternating series: *5 6* ↑ *7 8* ↑ *9* ? ↑
                          20   *19*   ?
12. Alternating series: *9 10* ↑ *11 12* ↑ *13* ? ↑
                           1   *2*   ?
13. Increases alternately by 2 (plus 2) then 3 (plus 3)—*4* (plus 2) *6* (plus 3) *9* (plus 2) *11* (plus 3) *14* (plus 2) *16* (plus 3) *19* (plus 2) ? (plus 3) ?
14. Alternating series: *8 8* ↑ *10 10* ↑ *12* ? ↑
                          1   *3*   ?
15. Alternating series: *14* ↑ *15* ↑ *16* ↑ ↑
                         1 2 *3 4*   ? ?
16. Alternating series: *10 12* ↑ *15 17* ↑ *20* ? ↑
                           50   *50*   ?
17. Alternating series: *1 2 3* ↑ *4 5 6* ↑ *7 8* ? ↑
                            50   *51*   ?
18. Increases alternately by (plus 1), (plus 2), (plus 1), (plus 3), (plus 1), (plus 4), etc.—*20* (plus 1) *21* (plus 2) *23* (plus 1) *24* (plus 3) *27* (plus 1) *28* (plus 4) *32* (plus 1) *33* (plus 5) *38* (plus 1) *39* (plus 6) ? (plus 1) ?

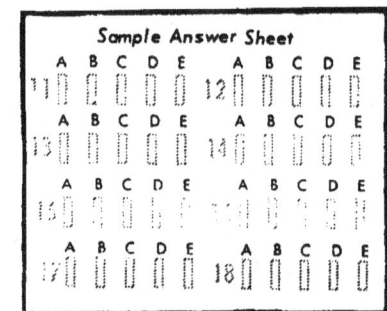

Sample Answer Sheet

The correct answers to the sample questions above are: 11A, 12C, 13A, 14B, 15D, 16D, 17B, and 18A.
On the test you will have *30 minutes* to answer as many of the 24 questions as you can.

DO NOT TURN THIS PAGE UNTIL THE TIME FOR THE SAMPLE QUESTIONS IS UP.

PART D

In each series below determine what the order of the numbers at the left is, and decide what the next two numbers should be. From the suggested answers at the right, choose the one that gives the next two numbers in the series and darken the box on the answer sheet with the same letter as your answer. (If the two numbers you have decided upon are not there, do the problem again.) Answer first the questions that are easiest for you; then answer the other ones.

Be sure to mark your answers in Part D of your answer sheet.

		A)	B)	C)	D)	E)
1.	8 9 10 8 9 10 8............	8 9	9 10	9 8	10 8	8 10
2.	3 4 4 3 5 5 3............	3 3	6 3	3 6	6 6	6 7
3.	7 7 3 7 7 4 7............	7 7	7 8	5 7	8 7	7 5
4.	18 18 19 20 20 21 22......	22 23	23 24	23 23	22 22	21 22
5.	2 6 10 3 7 11 4............	12 16	5 9	8 5	12 5	8 12
6.	11 8 15 12 19 16 23......	27 20	24 20	27 24	20 24	20 27
7.	16 8 15 9 14 10 13.........	12 11	13 12	11 13	11 12	11 14
8.	4 5 13 6 7 12 8............	9 11	13 9	9 13	11 9	11 10
9.	3 8 4 9 5 10 6 11 7........	7 11	7 8	11 8	12 7	12 8
10.	18 14 19 17 20 20 21......	22 24	14 19	24 21	21 23	23 22
11.	6 9 10 7 11 12 8.........	9 10	9 13	16 14	13 14	14 15
12.	7 5 3 9 7 5 11............	13 12	7 5	9 7	13 7	9 9
13.	7 9 18 10 12 18 13.........	18 14	15 18	14 15	15 14	14 18
14.	2 6 4 8 6 10 8............	12 10	6 10	10 12	12 16	6 4
15.	7 9 12 14 17 19 22.........	25 27	23 24	23 25	24 27	26 27
16.	3 23 5 25 7 27 9............	10 11	27 29	29 11	11 28	28 10
17.	18 17 16 14 13 12 10.......	9 8	6 7	8 6	8 7	10 9
18.	5 7 8 10 11 13 14 16.......	18 19	17 18	18 20	17 19	19 20
19.	28 27 25 24 22 21 19.......	18 16	17 16	18 17	17 15	20 18
20.	2 2 4 6 6 8 10............	12 12	12 14	10 10	10 8	10 12
21.	2 7 3 8 4 9 5............	6 7	10 6	6 10	10 11	5 10
22.	19 18 16 21 20 18 23.......	20 25	25 20	22 25	22 20	25 22
23.	3 5 7 7 4 6 8 8 5 7 9......	9 6	6 6	6 9	10 8	8 10
24.	15 26 24 16 21 19 17 16 14 18..	17 15	11 9	15 14	17 16	11 10

If you finish before the time is up, check your answers to Part D. Do not go to any other part.

CORRECT ANSWERS FOR CLERK-CARRIER TEST

www.ingramcontent.com/pod-product-compliance
Lightning Source LLC
Chambersburg PA
CBHW080731230426
43665CB00020B/2703